GOODBYE, ANTOURA

GOODBYE, ANTOURA

A MEMOIR OF THE ARMENIAN GENOCIDE

Karnig Panian

FOREWORD BY
Vartan Gregorian

TRANSLATED BY
Simon Beugekian

EDITED BY
Aram Goudsouzian

INTRODUCTION AND AFTERWORD BY
Keith David Watenpaugh

STANFORD UNIVERSITY PRESS
Stanford, California

Stanford University Press
Stanford, California

Longer versions of chapters 1-8 of this work were originally published in Armenian in 1992 under the titles *Antourayi Vorpanotseh* [*The Orphanage of Antoura*] by the Hamazkayin Armenian Educational and Cultural Society in Beirut, Lebanon, and *Housher Mangoutian yev Vorpoutian* [*Memories of Childhood and Orphanhood*] by the Catholicosate of the Great House of Cilicia in Antelias, Lebanon. Chapter 9 is developed from an unpublished manuscript and is original to Stanford University Press's edition.

Printed in the United States of America on acid-free, archival-quality paper

Library of Congress Cataloging-in-Publication Data available upon request.

ISBN 978-0-8047-9543-2 (cloth)
ISBN 978-0-8047-9634-7 (electronic)

Typeset by Bruce Lundquist in 10.25/15 Adobe Caslon Pro

CONTENTS

Foreword   vii
Vartan Gregorian

Introduction   ix
Keith David Watenpaugh

Chapter 1   Childhood   1

Chapter 2   Deportation   22

Chapter 3   The Desert   42

Chapter 4   The Orphanage at Hama   65

Chapter 5   The Orphanage at Antoura   78

Chapter 6   The Raids   98

Chapter 7   The Caves   120

Chapter 8   Goodbye, Antoura   144

Chapter 9   Sons of a Great Nation   167

              Afterword   185
              Keith David Watenpaugh

              Acknowledgments   189
              Houry Panian Boyamian

FOREWORD

Vartan Gregorian

The history of World War I is steeped in tragedy so fathomless as to sometimes seem impossible to comprehend. Millions died, both soldiers and civilians. Nation-states emerged; others were carved up, absorbed into neighboring regions, or simply—forcibly—had their name and borders erased from the world map. But if one looks back at this world conflict, a single word among all others asserts its right to define the underlying tragedy of this era, and that is *genocide*.

One of the tales arising from the seemingly unspeakable atrocities of genocide is given an extraordinarily strong voice in this memoir by Karnig Panian (1910–1989). Panian was a young child when he was caught up in the Armenian Genocide. With heartbreaking and yet affectingly poetic language, he brings the reader into his life as an orphan subjected to the daily abuse that inculcated a devil's bargain: *Forget who you are and we will let you live. You will always remain the "Other" but at least you will be alive, and for that you should be grateful.* This combination of outright slaughter and brute-force brainwashing was the first modern example of a kind of historical lobotomy meant to erase an entire people from the record of human existence. Thankfully, it did not work.

The publication of this book is timely because it comes on the eve of the centenary of the Armenian Genocide. And it is presented to us at a time when genocide and ethnic cleansing are not just isolated episodes but practiced almost routinely around the world. Indeed, genocide seems to be one of the great afflictions of the twenty-first century. In her recent book, *A Problem from Hell: America and the Age of Genocide*, Samantha Power, the current United States ambassador to the United Nations, references acts of genocide against Armenians, and later Jews, Cambodians, Iraqi Kurds, Rwandan Tutsis, and Bosnians, arguing it is "no coincidence that genocide rages on" when the world becomes indifferent, overloaded, perhaps, by endless images of atrocities that appear before our eyes in the relentless news cycle that assaults us twenty-four hours a day, seven days a week.

And therein lies the great importance of *Goodbye, Antoura*. It is a testimonial to the impossibility of denying the invaluable, eternal, and unalterable humanity of even a single child, and thus, by extension, of his family, his village, his people. Armenians and all those who were subsequently devastated by genocidal acts never simply constituted a political problem to be solved, were never a "category" to be eliminated for the supposed purpose of a greater good or design, never a mere millet to be allowed a measure of autonomy until it suited a greater power to crush it into nonexistence. Karnig Panian will not allow us to rationalize that kind of excuse for the idea that even a single individual's memory or identity can be taken from him. Bodies may be slaughtered, human beings bludgeoned and burned, but if even a single child survives, then memory survives as well. Memory cannot be assassinated. Truth cannot be denied. Karnig Panian survived, along with the revelatory truth of his story, and all of humanity is enriched by what he remembers and what he relates.

This is a remarkable and unforgettable book. It is an indispensable tool for awakening our consciences, restoring our collective sense of decency, and forging our solidarity with all those who have suffered the horrors of genocide. And it bears a message that must be heard: we can never let our guard down. We can never forgive or forget the suffering of all Karnig Panians, all over the world. That is the responsibility of humanity. It is the responsibility of each and every individual, as well.

INTRODUCTION

Keith David Watenpaugh

The problems of the Middle East today are in many ways a legacy of the events and the aftermath of World War I, which raged a century ago. The lasting memory of that war in Europe is the brutality and butchery on the Western Front, with its networks of muddy trenches adorned with razor wire; the war in the Middle East is not remembered for its pitched battles, but rather for the unremitting atrocity that left in its wake the destruction of entire communities and peoples, including the genocide of the ethnic Armenian citizens of the Ottoman state.

Karnig Panian's memoir draws us into the landscape of inhumanity that was the war in the Middle East. It unfolds against the deportation of his family as part of a campaign by the Ottoman state to destroy the community of Ottoman Armenians using the exigent circumstance of the war. This included the forced internal displacement of Panian and most of his family to an ill-supplied concentration camp just outside the city of Hama as Greater Syria (today's Lebanon, Syria, Jordan, Palestine, and Israel) itself was beset by a famine. Though blamed on successive waves of swarming locusts, that famine was created instead by the state's war effort and a lack of concern for civilian welfare. Just like the Great Leap Forward in China, it wasn't created by a natural disaster. Using the cover of the war, the Ottoman state took Panian and sought to annihilate his identity while it killed his family. And though the Ottoman state lost the war, the successor state, the ultranationalist Republic of Turkey, prevented him from returning home or certainly achieving any justice for what he had lost.

Although the role of World War I in shaping European culture and society has been the subject of scholarship for many years, only recently has the war's impact on the social history of the Middle East attracted much attention. This important turn toward the social history of the war—telling the story of children like Karnig Panian—has been the result of better access to archives and new historical techniques drawn from the study of gender, ethnicity, and the environment, but also of a commitment among younger scholars to bring the memoirs, art, music, journalism, and literature created by the Ottoman state's minorities—Greeks, Jews, Armenians, and Kurds—into the story of the war, which has been dominated by a focus on the nationalist narratives of the dominant Arab and Turkish communities.

This new approach has given us a much richer vision of the history of World War I in the Middle East, but also a deeper understanding of the enormity of the human cost of the conflict. It tells us that as the Ottoman state sought to regain its position in the Middle East and push back the armies of the British, French, and Russian empires, it embraced ideologies, policies, and systemic and structural violence that brought immense harm to its civilian populations, primarily those seen as possible impediments to the unity of the state and the dominance of the Turkish-speaking Sunni Muslim elite.

⌣

The genocide of the Ottoman Armenians (1915–1922), the first of the twentieth century's many genocides, took place in this crucible of wartime ideology and violence. Armenians were concentrated in several Eastern Anatolian provinces, where many worked farms or lived in villages and small cities. Still, they constituted a significant religious and linguistic minority throughout the Ottoman state and were woven into the fabric of Ottoman society as bureaucrats, intellectuals, artists, and businessmen. During the genocide entire villages, cities, and regions were emptied of their Armenian inhabitants: the women and children were internally displaced, often to concentration camps; the men were either killed at the outset or conscripted into forced labor battalions and executed sometime later. Many of the displaced were sent to the deserts of Syria, where they were subjected, by plan, to plunder, starvation, kidnapping, enslavement, rape, and murder.

During the war, the Ottoman state's military junta of modernizing nationalists—known in the West as the Young Turks—sought to reduce the percentage of ethnic Armenians in several provinces of the Ottoman Empire where they were the majority or plurality. The Young Turks reasoned that if the Armenian population in those particular provinces was reduced or eliminated altogether, calls for Armenian autonomy would be a non-issue after the war. And the integrity of the Ottoman state would no longer be threatened by the possibility of international intervention on the behalf of Armenians. Other motives included the destruction of a relatively successful Armenian middle class to make way for a national Turkish middle class: the confiscation of Armenian land and wealth benefitted the Ottoman state and Turkish merchants, bankers, and landowners. Likewise, the forced displacement and dispossession of Armenians provided opportunities to resettle the vast numbers of Turkic and Muslim refugees fleeing the Russian Empire and the Balkans. The fact that Armenians were a vulnerable religious minority in the empire played a role; however, questions of "race" and identity did not have the prominence they would have in the Holocaust.

An important exception to that conclusion first came to light as the forces of the Ottoman Empire retreated from Greater Syria in the autumn of 1918, when word that the state orphanage in the Lebanese town of Antoura had been abandoned by its Ottoman administrators reached the Beirut committee of the American Red Cross.

After traveling by automobile up the coast road, committee members, many of whom were affiliated with the Syrian Protestant College (later the American University of Beirut), were greeted with a remarkable sight. Nearly a thousand Armenian and four hundred Kurdish boys and few girls had been left without adult caregivers and were trying to run the orphanage themselves. The children were starving, and appeared to have been mal-nourished for a long time.

The Americans also learned that Antoura had been much more than a simple state orphanage. Rather, it was the site of an insidious social ex-periment inextricably linked to the Ottoman state's attempt to exterminate its Armenian population through genocide. The young people explained to the Americans that the administrators of the orphanage, some benign and some cruel, had sought to transform them by compelling them to convert to Islam, circumcising the boys, changing their Armenian names to Muslim names, forcing them to speak Turkish, and exposing them to nationalist indoctrination.

The orphanage at Antoura had been the brainchild of Jemal Pasha (1872–1922), one-third of the Ottoman Empire's ruling Young Turk junta and the military governor of Greater Syria, and Halide Edip (1884–1964). Halide Edip Adıvar was the leading Turkish feminist of her day. She had been the product of the American missionary educational project in the Ottoman state and had herself become deeply involved in wartime relief work through her professional association with the Ottoman Red Crescent Society and personal associations with the Young Turks.

Jemal Pasha had ordered that Armenian and Kurdish children be brought to the orphanage from throughout the region, usually from orphan-ages run by foreign missionaries. He had appointed the American-educated Halide Edip inspector for schools in Beirut, Damascus, and Aleppo. In that capacity she also administered the orphanage over a six-month period in 1916–1917, using it as a venue to implement new educational ideas drawn from her understanding of Montessori and the role of civic education to promote Turkish nationalism, which she planned to expand to the rest of the Ottoman state after the war.

What Halide Edip and Jemal Pasha had planned to achieve at Antoura was similar to what nineteenth- and early twentieth-century social reform-ers in the United States and Canada sought to accomplish with American Indian boarding schools, where Native Americans were forced to give up their cultural identity and assimilate with the dominate culture in the name of civilization and being "improved." In this case, Armenians, other Christian minorities such as Assyrians, and non-Turkish Muslim children (primarily Kurds) were supposed to be acculturated into the dominant group and become *Turks*; and indeed there was a great deal of support for the work at Antoura from the upper echelons of Ottoman society, who perceived it as merciful, charitable, and modernizing. Clearly, Halide Edip saw her role at the orphanage as a manifestation of an Ottoman "civilizing mission." The children in that orphanage were to emerge as modern *Turkish* citizens who, freed of what she considered their inferior Armenian and Kurdish identities, would join the national community and support the Ottoman state.

Motives aside, what Halide Edip did at Antoura constitutes genocide. Article 2, section E. of the 1948 Convention on the Prevention and Punishment of Genocide reads: "Genocide means any of the following acts committed with intent to destroy, in whole or in part, a national, ethnical, racial or religious group, as such: . . . Forcibly transferring children of the group to another group." The framers of the convention had in mind precisely the kind of organized and systematic efforts employed at the orphanage when they included this final element in the definition of the crime.* It is important to recognize that a standard element of late-Ottoman social policy had been to convert orphans regardless of origin in the state's care to Sunni Islam, the religion of the empire. However, during the genocide, the scope and policies of this orphanage and other Ottoman state orphanages expanded to such an extent that they must be distinguished from prewar state orphanages or those run by Christian missionaries, and certainly from those administered by international humanitarian organizations after the war.

Of course, the most distinctive feature of these wartime orphanages was that the Ottoman state itself was responsible for making the Armenian children orphans by killing their parents. In addition to Turkification at state orphanages, the genocide of the Ottoman Armenians witnessed a whole range of other techniques to transfer children: children were sold, bought,

---

* See my "'Are There Any Children for Sale?': Genocide and the Transfer of Armenian Children (1915–1922)," *Journal of Human Rights* 12:3 (2013): 283–95.

and stolen during episodes of mass killing and forced migration; they faced organized foster placement and loss of property and inheritance rights.

The turning over of the Antoura orphanage to the care of American relief officials as Ottoman authority melted away sheds light on the least understood part of this element of the crime of genocide: children's resistance to transfer and the loss of identity. As Bayard Dodge, a member of the faculty of the Syrian Protestant College and later president of the American University of Beirut, explained in a report at the end of the war, as soon as the management of the institution was placed in the hands of the American Red Cross in Beirut, "Immediately the Armenian children *asserted their rights*. They refused to use their Turkish names and they brought out Armenian books, which they had hidden away in secret places during the Turkish régime."[*] It is both remarkable and telling of the nature of identity that the young orphans, even subjected to the harsh discipline of Antoura, managed to save a part of themselves, the memory of their origins, and to safeguard and protect forbidden objects that connected them to their murdered parents and the communities from which they had been torn. The new American and Armenian caregivers of the orphanage immediately began to reconnect the young people to the Armenian community, fostering family reunification and organizing those who were orphaned into makeshift families of blended older and younger children, often overseen by a late-teenaged Armenian girl.

The process of reconnection—called in Armenian, *Vorpahavak*, "the gathering of orphans"—begun at Antoura was reproduced throughout much of the Ottoman state that was under foreign occupation at the end of the war. The Armenian General Benevolent Union, the League of Nations, and American Near East Relief—as well as individual Armenian families—worked to recover young people who had been transferred during the genocide. Sometimes this was accomplished by the repurchase of the children; at times, particularly in the Syrian desert, armed soldiers were

---

[*] Archives, American University of Beirut (1919), "Report from Bayard Dodge (Beirut) to C. H. Dodge (New York City) concerning the relief work in Syria during the period of the war," Folder AA: 2.3.2.28.3, Howard Bliss Collection 1902–1920, p. 13 (emphasis added).

called upon to intervene; in other cases young people rescued themselves as it were, making harrowing journeys across the desert to reach the relative safety of one of the League of Nations' several Rescue Homes that had been established to receive and rehabilitate the trafficked. The intake records of the Rescue Home in Aleppo, by far the largest, have been preserved by the United Nations. Those records include a short narrative of the young people from the time of the genocide until they entered the facility and document the kinds of violence and loss described by Panian in his memoir with unremitting consistency.[*]

In the Ottoman capital of Istanbul, the process of recovery was centered at an institution called the Neutral House.[†] It was a joint project of the League of Nations, the Ottoman Red Crescent, Armenian organizations, and ecclesiastical leadership. At the house, children whose identity was in dispute were observed by a team of representatives of the Armenian and Greek communities—either secular political officials or delegates of the respective patriarchates—a representative from the Ottoman Red Crescent Society, and advisors from the British government. Upon the determination of their status, they were returned to their community. Decisions about the fate of the children were made on the basis of the observations by these community representatives, who voted on each child. The children often arrived without documentation and the observers encouraged them to recall nursery rhymes and folk songs from their past to determine their origin. Very few, if any, of the disputed children were ever determined to be Muslim.

In the early 1920s the League of Nations dispatched investigators to better understand the facility's operations and decide whether similar houses could be established in the rest of the Ottoman state. In the course of their work, the investigators gained access to registries of Ottoman state orphan-

---

[*] Archives of the League of Nations, United Nations Organization, Geneva, Records of the Nansen International Refugee Office, 1920–1947, "Registers of inmates of the Armenian Orphanage in Aleppo," 1922–1930, 4 volumes.

[†] This discussion of the Neutral House is drawn in part from my "The League of Nations' Rescue of Armenian Genocide Survivors and the Making of Modern Humanitarianism, 1920–1927," *American Historical Review* 115:5 (December 2010): 1315–39.

ages, in which they noted that the names of Christian children had been overwritten with Muslim names.

They concluded that about half of all orphans in Istanbul, around five thousand children, were Armenian in origin, with another six thousand in other parts of Allied-occupied Anatolia. Moreover, the commissioners accepted as reliable a figure of 60,000 provided by the Armenian Patriarchate as the number of Armenian children still held in Ottoman orphanages and Muslim homes.

The Neutral House's program elicited strong resentment among Istanbul's elite, including Halide Edip, who had left Syria when Jemal Pasha resigned as military governor in 1917. Both had returned to Istanbul. Jemal Pasha fled the capital for Germany at the time of the Ottoman surrender. Tried in absentia for war crimes in Syria, he was killed in 1922 by Armenian operatives for his role in the genocide. Halide Edip took a leadership position in the Ottoman Red Crescent society, became active in Turkish nationalist politics, and later penned her memoirs.

Halide Edip's concerns about the Neutral House were the apparent illicit transformation of Muslim children into Armenians—the inversion of what she had done at Antoura. Indeed, it is in her writings about the situation of children in the postwar empire that Edip's hatred and distrust of Armenians is most pronounced; her writing has a texture similar to contemporary anti-Semitism in the way it casts Armenians as a mythical and existential enemy of the Ottomans, even to the point of borrowing tropes from blood libel and child cannibalism in describing a conspiracy to turn Turkish children into Armenians, thus also turning the accusations leveled against her for her work at Antoura back toward the Armenians themselves. Hence she complains, "when the children were brought in large numbers from orphanages of Anatolia they were sent to the Armenian church in Koum Kapou [Kumkapı], a hot-pot which boiled the Turkish children and dished them out as Armenians," and she concludes that "the children who were brought to the [Neutral House] were left in the care of the Armenian women, and these Armenian women either through persuasion or threats or *hypnotism*, forced the Turkish children to learn by heart the name of an

Armenian woman for their mother and the name of an Armenian man for their father."* As a motive, she provides no reason beyond fanaticism ("so far even the Christian missionaries could not go in their zeal") and dismisses the assertion of the "Armenians"—and implicitly the League's representatives—to the contrary because "the Moslem Turks do not have the missionary instincts of the Christians of the West."†

This rhetorical strategy of inversion—depicting the perpetrators of genocide as the real victim—is a constant trope of genocide denial. Moreover, her attitude takes on additional meaning in the face of a conclusion drawn in the report of League's observers that Halide Edip, in addition to her work at the Antoura orphanage and in conjunction with the Red Crescent Society, had been involved in a program to place large numbers of trafficked Armenian children from southeastern Anatolia and the province of Aleppo with elite and middle-class Ottoman Muslim families in Istanbul.

Modernizing Turkey and defending its Muslim elite against Western criticism are key elements of Halide Edip's life's work, but her reluctance to protect Armenian children or even voice empathy for them as victims of genocide shows a basic lack of human compassion. For Halide Edip questions of social distinction and religion placed limits upon the asserted universal nature of humanity; for her, genocide had not been too high a price to pay for Turkish progress, modernity, and nationalism.

❧

Karnig Panian, who was *held* at the Antoura orphanage during the last years of the war, wrote the memoir that follows.‡ We are extremely fortunate that it has now been translated into English and can be shared with a

---

* Halidé Edib [Halide Edip], *The Turkish Ordeal: Being the Further Memoirs of Halidé Edib* (New York: Century, 1928), 17 (emphasis added).

† Ibid., 16.

‡ Garnik Banean, *Husher mankut'ean ew orbut'ean* (Antelias, Lebanon: Kat'oghikosut'iwn Hayots' Metsi Tann Kilikioy, 1992) or *Memories of Childhood and Orphanhood*, is one of two extant autobiographical accounts of orphan life at Antoura, the other being the oral history of Harutyun Alboyajian collected by Verjine Svazlian, *The Armenian Genocide: Testimonies of the Eyewitness Survivors* (Yerevan: Gitutyun Publishing House, 2000).

broad audience of those interested not just in the Armenian Genocide, but all genocides and the history of children and childhood during war. It is a critical rejoinder to the elite and self-aggrandizing account of the orphanage written by the perpetrator Halide Edip in her 1926 English-language memoir. She justified the inherent inhumanity of that institution and others like it as merely wartime expediency. Unlike her writings, in which the victims are forced to stand silent, Panian's is a detailed and full-throated story of loss, resistance, and survival that is told without bitterness or overt sentimentality. His is a story as well of how even young children recognize injustice and can organize against it and form a sense of identity and belonging that they will fight to maintain. Even though he was a child at the time the events he describes in the memoir took place, he paints a painfully rich, accurate, and detailed picture of the lives and agency of Armenian orphans during the genocide. It is a remarkable contribution to the global literature of witness, as well a unique source for understanding the bitter years of the war and its aftermath through the eyes of one of its youngest and most vulnerable participants. From the perspective of modern Middle East history, the memoir is critical to understanding wartime civilian suffering and Armenian trauma and survival during and after the genocide; it is a unique tool to help the historian recover children survivors as discrete historical actors.

Panian's memoir also belongs to the emerging body of Armenian literature of human rights witness in English. It should become part of the broader global conversation about the nature of suffering and humanity. His look back to a childhood he was denied embodies the whole truth of the larger loss of humanity, or rather its theft, which makes genocide the crime of crimes. He recalls throughout his work moments that are reminiscent of passages in Primo Levi's reflections on his survival in the Auschwitz concentration camp during the Holocaust, *The Drowned and the Saved*, in the way he demands of his readers an unflinching look at the fragility of humanity in the face of deprivation, cruelty, and immense indifference.

In retrospect, Turkification was perhaps the least of the atrocities visited upon the young people at Antoura. Panian's survival and life after Antoura assures us that humanity, once denied, can be reclaimed.

GOODBYE, ANTOURA

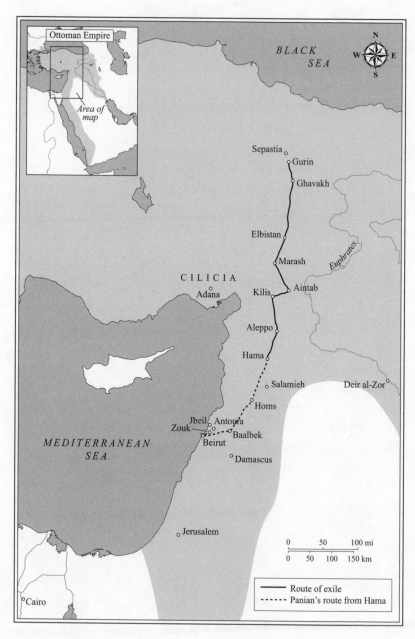

Karnig Panian's Journey

CHAPTER 1

CHILDHOOD

IT SEEMED TO ME that God had placed the Panians under his personal protection.

In our village of Gurin,[*] my grandfather had a vast, densely cultivated cherry orchard—an expanse of four thousand cherry trees! At least, they said four thousand, but who knew? Nobody had ever counted. Only my grandfather knew for sure. When asked about it, he would smile contentedly and say "Four thousand? More, much more!" For him, cultivating these trees was like an act of religious devotion. On a separate plot of land he had rows of apple, pear, peach, and apricot trees, and even more cherry trees.

On workdays, right after stepping out of the house, he would cast a fatherly glance toward the orchards before walking on. On Sundays, after Mass, he would go straight to his trees, even before stepping inside the house. He would gaze at the leaves, pick up the pebbles and rocks from the soil, and gather broken twigs. He would inspect the trunks to make sure that worms hadn't gotten into them. He would then cast a final glance over his dominion. Sighing contentedly, he would make his way back home, walking with his eyes looking at the ground. When he finally came in through the door, the

---

* Gurin, known in Turkish as Gürün, is in east central Anatolia.

lunch table would be ready for him, and we would all be sitting around it, awaiting his arrival.

During harvest, donkeys would carry our produce to the markets. The fruit pickers, who were usually Turks, would work from dawn to dusk. In the evenings, they would return to their homes with a basket of assorted fruit in their hands—the perk of their job, an extra privilege granted by my grandfather. The orchards produced enough to reward everyone with plenty.

My grandfather's gardens belonged to the entire extended family. Almost every day, this or that group of relatives would take a stroll through one of them. They would pick the ripened fruits and chat while their happy children played. My friends and I would compete to see who could collect the most tree sap, which seeped out of the trunks. We would eat it, and it would stick to our tongues and the roofs of our mouths. I remember the taste exactly—I liked it more than anything else in the world.

We also had a vegetable garden where we grew cucumbers and tomatoes, pumpkins and eggplants, lettuce and potatoes, onions and garlic, mint and beans. In another corner of our lands was a vast field of flowers, with rows of roses, lilies, carnations, daisies, and basil plants that intoxicated the air with their fragrance.

"It's an empty world, an empty world," Manug Emmi* would say to my grandfather. "It's up to us to fill it with homes, with fields, with beauty, and show God that we can create something out of nothingness."

"That's how it's been since the beginning," my grandfather would reply. "We build our homes, we plant our trees, we fill the Earth, but there are still those who struggle in misery, there are still beggars and thieves."

"When God created man, he created him to live in the Garden of Eden," mused Kevork Emmi from off to the side, "but beggars, thieves, and criminals have always existed, and will always exist. Such is the world, and it will never change. Cain and Abel, I tell you."

༄

---

* *Emmi* is a male honorific, translatable into "uncle."

My grandfather had always been God-fearing and pious. With his own hands he had built homes and a church, and he never missed a Sunday Mass at the local church. For decades he had sung the glory of God. He often participated in official rites, and when he toiled in the fields, he always murmured his hymns and prayers. He would sing in such wistful tones, with such a sweet voice. Sometimes I would try to sing along—mostly with the tune, as I didn't know the words. At night, right before going to sleep, I would once again hear the soft music coming from my grandfather, and I would doze off in my grandmother's arms.

I don't remember much about my father. I had very little awareness of being his son. He would leave early in the morning and return late at night. During our meals, he would talk sparingly of daily events, of the goings-on in town, and of neighbors and acquaintances. He rarely spoke of business. By trade, my father was a cobbler. He owned a shop in town and produced high-quality, expensive shoes. He even made Yemeni boots, preferred by Turks and Kurds. Several times during the year he would fill a bag with his shoes, and he would tour the nearby villages, sell his wares, and return with sacks of grain, rice, lentils, and beans, as well as jars of jam and honey.

My mother was the personification of love and joy. It seemed as if a gentle, kind star shone out of each of her eyes, and her expression conveyed a virtuous serenity. Her smile was like the shining sun, and it generously graced me, my sister, and my brother. She knew by heart every single one of the prayers recited at our church, and when she was working I often heard her sing hymns, too. She also knew all of the popular songs of the time, and she often sang them in her melodious voice. She was still young, and extremely beautiful, and she was always the talk of the neighborhood women. "There has never been a woman like her in our town, nor will there ever be one again," they would say.

My maternal grandmother lived with us. My father invited her after the death of her other daughter and the emigration of her son to distant lands. She helped around the house, mostly taking care of the children, satisfying some of her longing for her dead daughter and her distant son. At nights, we scarcely left her alone. My sister and my brother would sleep on her lap, and I would sleep leaning against her back. It seemed to me that she never slept. She spent the hours covering us with blankets and murmuring prayers over us. She was an old woman, exhausted by life, but her prayers gave her strength. She was our guardian angel, completely dedicated to her family.

My grandfather's wife, by contrast, was a disagreeable woman. She had appeared on the scene about a year after the death of my grandmother, and she had married my grandfather. She was already quite mature and there was no talk of her having any children. She seemed jealous of my mother and her three healthy, happy children. She refused to mend my grandfather's pants and socks, and she didn't set up a good table like the other women of the family. She never had a smile on her face, never had a kind word for us like everybody else. She barely ever left the house or had any visitors, instead remaining ensconced in her room like an owl, whiling away the days.

∽

It was Sunday—a clear, bright, beautiful day. Birds sang above the flower-speckled field. We could almost feel the soil breathing, the trees growing. From the distance, we heard the tolling of the church bells. The ceremonies inside the church had started long ago. It seemed like the pealing bell was admonishing latecomers and rushing them toward the church doors.

That day, our entire extended family went to church. Nobody was left at home. My grandfather led our procession, alongside the other men of the family, followed by the women and children. My sister sat on the shoulders of my cousin Krikor, and my brother and I held my mother's and grandmother's hands. We observed this tradition every Sunday, both in the heat of summer and the frosts of winter, according to the wishes of my grandfather.

Naturally, we children understood little of the church ceremony. Whenever people crossed themselves, my mother would squeeze my hand and I would imitate the grown-ups. The adult men gathered right before the altar, comfortable on divans and plush rugs, where they would occasionally fall to their knees, bow toward the floor, then stand back up and cross themselves. The women and children crammed into the balcony of the church, where they prayed and sang their subdued hymns. There was something melancholic in the words of the priest. I'm not sure anybody in town understood his elaborate sermons, but there was no mistaking the almost hopeless tone in his voice. When he spoke, sadness inexplicably enveloped my soul. I would begin suffocating, and I would pray that the ceremony would end soon. At such times, my mother would nudge me, admonishing me to keep quiet.

My eyes darted about. I sometimes looked toward the altar, sometimes up into the steeple, and other times toward the colorful tinted windows that threw shards of hues upon the congregation below.

When the ceremony ended, we formed a long line to kiss the priest's Bible. Aping my parents and grandparents, I, too, kissed the Bible, without understanding what I was doing. Finally, we left the church and headed back home. The adults exchanged blessings, laughed, and chatted joyfully.

The entire extended family gathered back at our house. Today, all the Panians were going to the spring beyond my grandfather's orchard.

My mother and my uncle's wife, Hnazant, had spent the whole previous day cooking. They had affixed flattened balls of dough against the red-hot walls of the smoking earthen *tonir*,* and then, a few minutes later, extracted baked loaves of bread and arranged them on large trays, filling the air with the smell of baked dough. Then they brought out a huge cauldron of *herisa*,† lowered it into the tonir, and shut the lid of the cauldron tight, so that no steam escaped. That night, they kept uncovering the tonir and extracting the huge cauldron, stirring the boiling stew with a ladle.

A large stick was put through two notches of the cauldron. Two young men lifted it out of the tonir and carried it up on their shoulders. Other food and drinks were packed into baskets, and then we headed out again. It was like a wedding procession, led by the two young men carrying the herisa. On our right side was a thin stream that gurgled along the orchards. To our left was a steep cliff, and at the bottom of it was the running river. The procession advanced along this thin path—one wrong step would send us

---

* An oven dug into the earth, commonly found in kitchens in nineteenth-century Asia Minor.
† A stew made with crushed wheat and beef or poultry.

rolling down the cliff. But we joked and talked, and it seemed like a festival. The children filled the air with giggles.

Occasionally, our procession would halt, and the young men carrying the cauldron would be replaced. The children ran ahead, fell behind, rolled down the hill, and even fell into the water, their joyful shrieks splitting the air.

The adults' conversations revolved around the children, who would soon be the pillars of their family—masters of the homes, orchards, and fields. More attention was paid to the boys. After all, the girls would someday be married off and become part of another family, another household.

"They've had a good start to life. We'll see what fate has in store for them," mused Kevork Emmi. He philosophically puffed his tobacco smoke, and through its folds he glared at the children in the vale.

The stream ran through the valley, lined by lush carpets of green grass dotted with colorful flowers, sucking up the rays of the sun. This corner of our town was called Tsakh Tsor, or, in the jargon of our neighborhood, Jakh Chor. It was a corner of paradise, a unique natural treasure. The valley gradually narrowed toward a small spring fed by two streams of water cascading from the icy, snow-clad mountains above. At the head of the spring was a huge pool, made of flat stone, with water as clear as the sky and surrounded by giant, bending willows. The water rushed into the valley, creating rainbows in the hovering mist.

Near the pool was a large, empty field. We settled ourselves in the cool shadows, sitting on small rugs, the stream's mist caressing our cheeks. Men and women alike headed for the pool, where they splashed and drank the icy water until their stomachs almost burst. Children ran about the pool and sprayed each other with water. All this created the sense of a surreal dream, into which I slipped comfortably.

While we played with abandon, our grandfathers sat in a tight circle, having a very serious discussion. The main speaker was my grandfather—his voice was the loudest. His brothers, Sahag and Manug, listened without saying a word, like marble statues.

"This spring is too small. We've got to enlarge it. We need to buy more of the land around it. We'll take some soil from the mountain, and then make a bridge linking this side of the stream to the other. There, we'll plant another orchard. As for this area—there are a hundred and twenty-five of us and we can barely all sit together at the same time. We need to enlarge the field, too—it needs to fit at least five hundred people." My grandfather would have continued, had he not been interrupted by Kevork Emmi.

"How many years will it take to do all this? Ten? Twenty?"

"I'll start. Those who survive me can finish it."

"When will the Panian dynasty reach five hundred people?" asked a skeptical Vartan Emmi.

"This is *our* land. It was left to us by our ancestors, and it's our duty to multiply the wealth they bequeathed to us, so that the next generations can enjoy it," replied my grandfather. "I believe in this mission, and I want you all to believe in it, too. And don't you forget—the Armenian nation will prosper again, thanks to those who always strive for more, not those who are content with what they were given. Let me finish this government *seray*.* After that, I'm not taking on anything new. I'll hire a few Turkish workers and we'll get to work. This day next year, when we all gather here again, much will be different."

"Well, first we've got to find out if they'll even let us do it. The Turks have their eyes on these lands," said Serop Emmi, who had been smoking silently this entire time.

"If we believe everything those bastards say, we'll never get anything done," retorted my grandfather. "Our ancestors came from Akoulis† two or three hundred years ago and settled on this land. We built our homes, our churches, and we tended to our fields. My own orchards took thirty-five, forty years out of my life. I made my money, I bought my lands, I grew my crops. My cherry orchard didn't spring out of the soil. I had to buy it piece by piece, then work like a slave for each acre of it. Tree by tree, bush by bush, I finally got where I am." He was inspired. He was overwhelmed with emotion.

As the women unpacked food, a squad of young men competed to see who could best beat the still-intact grains of wheat in the herisa until they

---

* A government building, or the building in which a government official has his quarters

† A village of Sasoun, the mountainous area southwest of Lake Van and west of Bitlis.

were all melted away. *Hareh! Hareh! Herisa!*[*] they sang as they went about their work. Beside them was a large sack of butter, which would be melted atop the herisa.

The rugs were arranged in a circle around the pool. Each family had brought its own cushions and pillows, as well as large packages of delicacies. The buttery herisa was now ready. Wives from each household used deep ladles to fill their vats with the stew, and then they scooped up a healthy amount of butter. The vats were placed in the center of each household's group. Everyone was to eat from the same vat. The young brides of the family hovered around the groups, filling glasses with wine. But before emptying them, everyone waited for my grandfather's words.

He stood up, took his fez off his head, and handed it to the closest woman in his circle. He then raised his eyes to the sky and asked God to bless the entire Panian clan—the young and the old, the healthy and the sick. He implored God to always keep watch over the family, as he had done for so many years, and to lead all Panians down the path of virtue and piety. He then crossed himself and raised his glass of wine to his mouth, emptying it in one gulp. All the rest followed, and soon the only sound in the valley was the clinking of the spoons and glasses. With the warm wine coursing through their veins, the revelers began singing. As some played the *saz* and *kamancheh*,[†] popular songs succeeded one another in quick succession.

The plates of herisa were refilled, and bottles of wine and *oghi*[‡] were emptied. Though each family was gathered in its own space, each was a unit in the intricate pattern that was our clan. Good wishes and blessings were shouted across large distances, and joy dominated the valley.

Some of our neighbors arrived on the scene. "Welcome, welcome! Be our guests!" rang out from every corner, as every family made room for the newcomers. The newcomers offered songs, jokes, and graceful dances accompanied by the saz. I had never witnessed such a joyful feast.

---

[*] The words of a folk song often sung during the preparation of herisa.

[†] The saz is a long-necked stringed instrument of the lute family; the kamancheh, a bowed string instrument played by placing its tail on one's knee.

[‡] *Oghi* can refer to any of various alcoholic drinks, including raki or arak, that might be distilled from fruits or grains.

The vats of herisa disappeared, replaced by trays of pastries and fruit. Those who still had room in their stomach ate a few pieces. The sun was already slanting toward the horizon. The young brides jumped to their feet and began gathering the leftovers in their baskets, but the music, dancing, jokes, and children's games continued until darkness fell.

We finally started back to our homes. From beyond the summit of the hill facing us, the moon's half-helmet appeared, like a lantern suspended in the sky, guiding the revelers back home through the darkness.

◡

"My dear! You will go to school, and you will become a *man*!" my mother used to tell me. "If you study well, if you learn how to read and write, you'll never have to bend before anyone in life. Soon you'll learn to read the Nareg.* Soon you'll be reading the Bible! And not next year, but the year after, your little brother will be five years old and he'll be going to school, too! You've got to make sure you set a good example for him."

My father had become literate, and he attributed his success in life to that fact. On Sundays, after church and lunch, when we kids played, my father would pick up one of the huge, thick books from the top of his closet shelf, open it on his lap, and then, for a long time, lose himself in its pages. Sometimes, he would end up falling asleep with the book still open on his lap.

My mother, too, had a small prayer book, and at nights, right before putting out the lamp, she'd read a few pages of it, then kiss it reverently, hold it against her breast, and sleep with it under her pillow.

I started school when I was five years old. They gave us a notebook, a pencil, and a small, thin primer that was supposed to teach us how to read. Every morning, I would go to school convinced that I would learn how to read very soon. Every evening, I would return home and sit and stare at the pictures in my primer.

At our school, which was located in the shadow of the church, all of the students were boys and all of our teachers were male; women had never

---

* A prayer book compiled by St. Gregory of Nareg. It is one of the staples of the Armenian Church liturgy.

stepped inside the building. Our teacher was a rotund man. The ends of his ample mustache were always coiffed and rolled upward. He may have inspired some with fear due to his bulk, but in reality he was gentle. He never raised a hand to a child. Even though he carried a large ruler, he never used it to strike us. If we got too rowdy, he would strike his desk, but only to restore order in the classroom. He never hit us, even though quite a few of the boys were very mischievous. These were healthy, happy boys, with young blood coursing through their veins. Mischief dripped from their eyes.

When the weather was good, most of our hours were spent outdoors singing, dancing, and doing calisthenics. But the older boys clearly did real class work. We would hear the voice of their teacher explaining the lessons, or sometimes the voices of the boys reading aloud.

In the courtyard outside of school, some of the older students, instead of playing, would read their books, reviewing their lessons before going to class. This impressed me—those books must have been so important, divulging so many incredible and interesting secrets!

On Saturdays, we would file out of school and right into the church, finding the usual elderly worshippers there. Walking up the nave, we would cross ourselves and approach the altar. The priest on duty was a member of the Panian dynasty—Father Azken. The older boys of our school read the psalms and participated in the church service, resplendent in their clean, white shirts. Occasionally, the priest would raise his hands and bless the crowd. The ceremony would end with a recitation of the *Hayr Mer*.*

One Saturday, while we were still in the building and lining up to file into church, our schoolmaster stood on a small chair to make an announcement. He had a distraught expression. With a sad voice, he said that it was the last day of the school year. After church, we would all have to go home and not come back.

The students exchanged stunned, disbelieving glances. The schoolmaster's words were ominous, and the teachers around us had weary and anxious expressions.

---

* The Lord's Prayer. *Hayr Mer* literally means "Our Father."

Classroom by classroom, we went into the church, which swelled with worshippers. The atmosphere inside was stifled and dreary. Instead of plunging us into deep, reverent meditation, the hymns and the fragrant smoke of the incense created an oppressive atmosphere. After the ceremony, my cousin Krikor and I began our walk home.

Housewives hanging their laundry from their balconies eyed us warily. "Why are you going back home so soon? Is something the matter?" Krikor told them what happened.

By that evening, the news had spread all over town. Everybody had an opinion as to why it had occurred. There were strange fears and suspicions that the government was reverting to its old ways; it had massacred thousands of Armenians in the past, and perhaps now it was preparing to do the same. Survivors from previous pogroms had terrible premonitions. Rumors circulated among the Turks: Armenian revolutionaries had infiltrated the town, brought weapons with them, held a special meeting, and murdered a large number of Turks on the road. The bodies were discovered, but nobody knew how they had been killed; the government immediately alleged that the Armenian partisans were behind this heinous act.

"The massacres of 1895 and those of Adana in 1909* started just like this, too!" fretted Vartan Emmi, who styled himself as an expert on these issues. "It's true, the Ittihadist government seems a bit smarter, they seem to respect Armenians more, but scratch the surface, and you'll find the same wicked Turk underneath."†

Later that evening, my father arrived home and kissed his children. He caressed my mother's cheek and whispered in her ear. He joked with his children, trying to unburden his mind, but he ate his dinner in silence, and later that night, after my brother and sister went to bed, he and my mother

---

* In 1895, some three hundred thousand Armenians were killed on the orders of Sultan Abdul Hamid II, in part to alter the demographics of the eastern *vilayets* (provinces), in which Armenians formed either the majority or the plurality of the population. In 1909, one year after the restoration of the Ottoman Constitution, around thirty thousand Armenians were killed in the city of Adana and the surrounding region.

† The Ittihadist government refers to the *İttihat ve Terakki Cemiyeti*—the Committee of Union and Progress, also known as the Young Turks—which deposed the sultan in 1909 and eventually went on to plan and execute the genocide of the Armenians, beginning in 1915.

spoke in hushed tones. I tried to eavesdrop on them, but I couldn't understand much of what they said.

The next day, a Sunday, my grandfather, his brothers Manug and Sahag,
and Krikor and his mother came to our home. They started discussing the
closure of the school and the rumors surrounding the event. My grandfather's brothers had not heard the news. Stunned, they asked Krikor what
had happened, and he repeated the words of the schoolmaster.

A long silence ensued. There was nothing to say, or perhaps the men
were too stunned to speak. Was it an omen of worse things to come? In
their long lives, they had experienced many such events, and they had
learned that the closing of village schools usually presaged much worse.

〜

Manug Emmi was typically a gregarious, talkative man. He exhaled thick
clouds of smoke, like a chimney in mid-winter, and coughed endlessly. He
often yelled and even swore at his Turkish workers. He was not merely
pious; he was a religious zealot. At any given moment, he was ready to
lay down his life to defend his Armenian Apostolic faith. This was known
throughout the village, both by Armenians and by Turks. According to one
story, a few Armenian *aghas** once came from a distant part of our town to
visit Manug Emmi and my grandfather. They were Catholics, and they had
come to ask the two brothers to build a Catholic church. The two brothers
chased them out with insults: "A church? For you? You bastards, we'll build
a mosque for the Turks before we build a church for you heretics. Get out,
and don't ever come back again!"†

One morning, a few weeks after the closure of the school, Manug Emmi
failed to visit our house in the morning and greet my mother as usual. My
grandmother went out and learned that he was sick, and then my mother
left to see him. When she returned, her expression betrayed her troubled

---

* Leaders, or village chiefs.
† Most Armenians belong to the national Apostolic Church. Catholic Armenians (converted
 by missionaries) were often considered apostates and viewed as un-Armenian. Those views
 were likely reinforced by the Ottoman *millet* system, which categorized only Armenians who
 adhered to the national church as belonging to the Armenian *millet*.

thoughts. "He's got a very high fever," she said. "He can't even lie in bed, he's tossing and turning. They've tied pieces of potatoes to his forehead, and they've put his feet in hot water to fight off the illness."

Later that day, a host of older family members—men and women— headed toward Manug's house. He was one of the patriarchs of the clan; respect had to be paid to him and to his family. The only one missing was my grandfather's wife.

Then came the Ezajis, the shamans of the Caucasus, making fantastic claims regarding their healing powers. They worked hard on Manug, whose fever would sometimes subside. He would open his eyes and attempt to talk, and he would even try to smile at us. But soon he would faint again and fall back against the bed, and his fever would rise to new heights.

Soon he grew pale, started hallucinating, and became delusional. As time went on, he weakened considerably. Despair settled in everyone's hearts. The Nareg and the Bible were placed beneath his head. Father Azken blessed the sickbed. A Turkish doctor examined his mouth, chest, and back, listening to his pulse and breathing. As he left, he said, "We've done all we can. The rest is up to God. You must keep praying." He mounted his horse, a well-practiced expression of mourning plastered on his face.

Now despairing, the family turned to the wizened matriarchs of the Panian dynasty for salvation. These women did their best, too—they con- cocted herbal remedies and rubbed ointments all over Manug Emmi's back, chest, and forehead.

Over the next few weeks, the adults stood vigil. In the mornings, my grandmother would visit the sick man; in the afternoons, my mother did the same. They spoke to the unresponsive Manug Emmi, prayed fervently, cried, and returned home with swollen eyes. My grandfather and Sahag Emmi visited the sickbed every night after work, sitting with their dying brother, silently hoping that God would somehow work a miracle.

Manug Emmi's wife and daughters-in-law were in shock. What could they do? Despair weighed down upon them like a heavy stone.

One morning, Father Azken came to Manug Emmi's house to admin- ister the last rites.

We were too young to understand everything that was going on, so my brother and I played with my friends Garo and Sahag. Since the school was closed, we wandered through the orchards and fields all day. We could go wherever we wanted, play whatever games we wanted. I gazed around me— at the stream I knew so well, at the fields, at the distant mountains beyond which I knew nothing.

It was past noon when we returned home. The place was deserted. Even my mother and my grandmother were gone, and they had taken my baby sister with them. The hours passed. The shadows of the trees were getting longer. I was becoming impatient. My brother and I weren't hungry, but, still, we grew frustrated with this extended absence of any adult from the house.

Then I spied a procession coming our way. It was headed by my grandmother, who had my little sister in her arms, followed by my aunt and mother. They all walked with their eyes glued to the ground, dejected and tearful. My mother was sobbing. I asked her what was wrong.

"It's all over now . . . All over . . . " she replied with a choking voice. "Manug Emmi is no longer among us."

The next morning, Manug Emmi's house was invaded by a mass of people. There were Father Azken, another priest, all the men and women of the extended family, neighbors and friends, and even some local Turks. They murmured prayers, sang hymns, and filled the house with the smoke and smell of incense. They also brought a wheelbarrow and lay Manug Emmi atop it. The procession headed for the cemetery, passing through our courtyard. It was led by the priests, my grandfather, and my father, all followed by a host of known and unknown faces. People wailed and sobbed, and many women beat their breasts. My brother and I watched from behind our front door. When the entire crowd had passed, we finally gathered up the courage to go outside. The cemetery was usually one of our playgrounds, but for a few days, we were forbidden from playing there.

In the coming days, an endless procession of people came to our home to express their condolences. Clearly, the loss of Manug Emmi had affected not just his family, but the entire town. I started thinking that my great-

uncle was perhaps more than just a regular man. He was a man of honor
and achievements, and he would not be forgotten quickly.

A week later, a requiem service was held in the morning at our neighborhood church, the same church that had been built by my grandfather
and Manug Emmi. At noon, a meal was hosted in honor of the dearly
departed, beneath the great chestnut tree in our courtyard. Everybody ate,
drank, and blessed the soul of the dead. They spilled wine and oghi onto the
ground so that the departed could partake as well.

A few days later, life had almost returned to normal. Everyone was back
to his or her own work, his or her own world.

For days on end, whether I was alone at home or playing outside with
my friends, a thousand questions popped up in my mind, questions for
which I had no answers: What was death? What did it mean? And why did
it engender so much grief and fear in the souls of the living?

Though I stopped asking these questions after a while, things would never
be exactly the same. The departed was a patriarch of the family, whose shadow
had sheltered all of us, young and old, men and women. The departure of such
a man was bound to have serious consequences for the entire clan.

❧

Two or three months after Manug Emmi's death, our tears of sorrow transformed into tears of joy: two of my uncles, Stepan and Hagop, were coming
to town to visit their parents and kin. Both of these uncles were members
of the Ottoman army. Uncle Stepan had the rank of major, while Uncle
Hagop was a captain.[*]

They were the third and fourth children of my grandfather. I was so
proud that I had two uncles who were such high-ranking officers, and for
hours I would stare at their photographs, which hung in gilded frames in
our living room.

---

[*] Before the Young Turk Revolution of 1908, non-Muslims of the Ottoman Empire tended not
to serve in the Ottoman military. After the revolution, the Ottoman Empire included more
non-Muslims. Non-Muslim officers, especially in the Medical Corps, became more common.
In the months leading up to the genocide, Armenian soldiers were disarmed and organized
into labor battalions. With the onset of genocide, most Armenian soldiers were executed.

In our house as well as at my grandfather's, their imminent arrival was the only topic of conversation. Every night, we expressed hope that my uncles would arrive soon.

One day, my grandfather, father, and aunt asked me and my brother to get ready for a journey. Riding on the back of a carriage, we left the safety of our town and entered a new world. We had crossed the borders that had delineated my universe, and I found myself on a novel planet. I could see the endless valleys, the gigantic fields that dwarfed anything we had in our own town. The mountains were now much closer, much more tangible, much more awe-inspiring.

We reached a village called Ghavakh. Its population was mostly Armenian, and we even had some relatives living there. When we stopped in a courtyard, dozens of people welcomed us. Our hosts set up the supper table, bringing us whatever they had—bread, different kinds of cheese, fried eggs, honey, apricot and raspberry jam, fruit juices.

After the meal, the adults were engaged in conversation, so my brother and I wandered out of the house. Nearby, a flock of sheep were grazing, and around them were several chickens, pecking at the dirt. Some distance away, a lethargic dog was tied to a tree and slumbering in its shade. The horizon was a craggy collection of mountain peaks. To one side of the fields below was a thick forest, and we could hear the cacophony of thousands of chirping birds. How many more fields, valleys, and mountain chains were there to see? Would I be fortunate enough to explore this huge world? My imagination soared beyond our little corner of the universe.

When I went back inside, the living room was filled with tobacco smoke and passionate debate. Even the grandmothers were smoking or snuffing tobacco. The women in this village seemed to be more hardy and rougher than those in ours.

News came that there was a dust cloud above the road in the distance. My father went outside to check and then ran back in.

"They're here! They're here!" Chaos erupted. Everyone ran out into the courtyard. My grandfather, squinting his eyes, tried to spot the travelers in the distance. The dust cloud slowly came closer and closer, and after five or ten minutes, three carriages entered the village.

My uncles had finally arrived. They alighted from the carriages and into the arms of their relatives. The hugs and kisses lasted many minutes. After embracing my father, they lifted my brother and me into their arms and kissed us again and again.

Both of my uncles were dressed in their uniforms. They looked as resplendent as kings with their hats, their coats with shiny buttons, and the gold stars on their shoulders.

They wanted to get back to our town as soon as possible—they were impatient to see the rest of the family. My brother and I rode with my uncles back to Gurin. As we rode, I kept glancing furtively at my newfound relatives—their ruddy, healthy faces and expressions filled me with pride.

Finally, we came to a halt right outside our house. We were welcomed by my grandfather's wife, by my mother with my sister in her arms, and by a crowd of men and women from our extended family. They welcomed my uncles with embraces, kisses, and cries of joy.

Then we went into my uncle's house for coffee, fruit, and desserts. After the well-wishers were all gone, we sat around the table, enjoying the delicious dishes my mother had prepared for the occasion.

"A thousand welcomes to you, my sons," said my grandfather, raising his glass. "I thank God for allowing me to see this day, to finally welcome you back home." The men emptied their glasses and the women refilled them.

"Prosper and multiply, my children! Fill the world with more of our kind, and expand our family!" continued my grandfather. Then he fell silent.

There was something so powerful in his sudden silence that the toast failed to raise our spirits. Instead, everyone fell into a sort of gloom. My grandmother and mother had tears in their eyes.

The family had just buried Manug Emmi, and despite my grandfather's words, our future—the future of the children—was looking more and more uncertain.

My grandfather constantly said that his final wish before dying was to build two nice houses with gardens on the land adjacent to his house, where Hagop and Stepan could live and start their own families. They were respected, had good careers in the military, and had reached the appropriate age to settle down with wives of their own. Quite a few pretty girls were on the short list of possible matches. News spread through town that Hovhannes Emmi was looking for honorable brides for his two sons—and few families in town would refuse their daughter's hand if asked.

However, my uncles didn't stay in town for long. Only two weeks after their arrival, they had to leave again for the town where they were stationed. Those two weeks were among the best in my young life. Wherever my uncles went, they took me with them. I was proud of being their nephew. It felt like the brilliance of their uniforms, buttons, and shoes shined upon me.

My father had often spoken about how he wanted me to become a cobbler, while my mother preferred to have me enter the ranks of the clergy. But once I saw my uncles in their splendid uniforms, the idea of becoming a cobbler or a priest seemed laughable to me. All I could think of was how great it would be if I, too, joined the army and became an officer. At the time, I didn't consider that being a soldier meant being ready to kill and be killed.

༄

One night, we heard a commotion from the vegetable garden. The chickens in the henhouse filled the air with shrieks, as if they were fighting among themselves. The noise woke me up, and I saw that my mother and father were already on their feet, heading toward the door.

My father stormed out and ran down the stairs. Within a few seconds we heard sounds of yelling and running feet. We went to the balcony, which overlooked the henhouse. We could see two men running away from it. My father didn't bother chasing the thieves. After following them for a few seconds, he retraced his steps, closed the door of the henhouse, then came back upstairs.

"I know who they are," murmured my father. He had recognized the Turkish men who had worked for us in the fields.

"It's better to keep our mouths shut," suggested my grandmother. My mother, from the corner, nodded her approval.

"If we keep quiet, they'll only do worse," protested my father. "We need to teach them a lesson, so they'll stay away!"

"I'm scared of the evil those Turks can do to us," said my mother, her voice shaking with anxiety.

The next morning, we went down to the vegetable garden to assess the damage. The vegetables—tomatoes, cucumbers, onions, pumpkins—had all been crushed and trampled. The thieves hadn't been satisfied with that; they had also stolen a few chickens after decapitating them and tossing the heads on the ground. At the entrance of the henhouse, the floor was covered with the remains of dozens of crushed eggs.

"I still don't understand why they would do such a thing," mused my father. Nothing like this had ever happened before.

"This is not a good sign," replied my grandmother. "The Turks are getting restless again."

We spent that night on the balcony, as if trying to guard our home and our lands. We kept our eyes on the vegetable garden and the fields. "Things like this have never happened in our town," said my father. The Armenian neighborhoods, church, and school were all separated from the Turkish side of town. Not a single Turkish family lived on our street. Yet many Turks worked in our orchards or as servants in other wealthy Armenians' homes. They spoke Armenian as well as any of us did. At the town market, Armenian and Turkish merchants worked side by side without any disputes, and often with pleasure.

Yet my friends often referred to Turks as thieves, lazy, uneducated, or murderers. When my friends and I played together underneath the giant chestnut tree in the orchards, our favorite game was *vek*, dropping sticks or bones that foretold the player's future. We would play it to determine who was hungry, who had a full belly, or who was a thief. One time, when my friend dropped the vek, it fell in a way that indicated he was a thief. "You're a Turk! You're a Turk!" yelled my other friends, bursting with laughter.

But this was no game. The black hand of crime and thievery had descended upon our own home. As a child, I could sense the insecurity in the air. Until now, our doors had always remained open throughout the year and at all hours of the day and night. From then on I knew that our doors would remain locked all night.

"Crimes like this occurred constantly before the events of '95," recalled my grandmother. "Every morning, we'd wake up and hear of robberies, murders, and other crimes that had happened in the neighborhood. Overnight, Armenians and Turks who had lived in peace side by side turned into enemies. The thieves were always Turks or Kurds. So many of them were caught, but the other Turks always protected them."

"And," she added, "those isolated crimes eventually led to the massacres."

The next afternoon, officials in uniforms showed up at our door. They spent hours in the vegetable garden, examining every inch of the ground, presumably looking for evidence. They also carefully investigated the henhouse, the trampled vegetables and fruits, and the branches that the thieves had broken as they had made their escape. Then they found sets of footprints leading toward the valley, in the directions of the criminals' escape route. They painstakingly recorded everything, and after hours of detective work they confidently stated that it was a common break-in.

"Master Hovhannes," one of the officials said to my grandfather, "I assure you, within a few days we'll arrest the thieves and bring them here to you, with their arms and legs tied behind them." He and his colleagues stayed for another couple of hours, had some coffee, whiled away the time in easy conversation, then left.

The reason behind the government's supposed concern was the stature of my grandfather in the community, even in the eyes of the Turks. They, too, had benefited from his talent. He had constructed many government buildings, as well as many houses for the area's wealthy Turks.

A few days went by, and the thieves were still at large. A week later, the local authorities had forgotten all about it.

∽

During the warm summer nights, we slept on our roof, in the open air. My grandmother arranged the sheets and pillows, and after dinner we went up to the roof and got into our improvised beds. The apricot and plum trees gently swayed. Above us was only the sky, with its canopy of winking stars. Sometimes the moon reached the peaks of the nearby mountains and stared directly at us with her one keen eye. On clear nights, we rarely went to sleep right away. My brother and I engaged in horseplay well into the night, while our sister watched us and snickered. I felt like I could just extend my hand and pick the stars out of the sky, one by one. They were like gems inviting me to collect them. When I closed my eyes, I felt myself floating toward them, and I heard the mysterious, silent music they played in the ether.

I opened my eyes to the majestic sun rising above the mountains and embracing the world. Our cat, which usually slept near my sister, approached and rubbed against me, wishing me a good morning in her own way. I petted her, stretched my legs, and went downstairs into the house with the cat at my heels, as my mother was preparing breakfast.

My father had already gone to work. We sat and ate with the appetite of growing children—bread, cheese, jam, milk, and a large omelet. After the meal, my mother crossed herself and thanked God for the bounty of food. Armed with her blessings, we ran out to play with our friends.

We children had already forgotten the robbery and the distress it had caused. The sun was shining, and the days were long and warm. We lived comfortably and peacefully, deluded into thinking we were safe.

CHAPTER 2

DEPORTATION

IT WAS A HOT, DRY DAY in the summer of 1915 when the terrible news broke, causing communal outbursts of grief: the Ottoman government had declared a general mobilization, and all able-bodied men above a certain age were to be drafted into the army.

A few evenings later, my father came home, looking very upset. An edict had been issued that all men of military age had to present themselves to the town's recruitment center within a week. Over the next few days, my father emptied his store. He sold all of his merchandise to local Turks and handed over the keys to his apprentice. He had to go.

For my mother, it seemed like the sky had fallen. My grandmother was in a catatonic state, barely able to speak. The other young and middle-aged men of our extended family were also preparing to leave. The entire clan was thrown into chaos. Men spoke in hushed whispers in the corners. Dark rumors spread with lightning speed and panic overwhelmed all our hearts.

Men of all creeds and religions had been called up for the armed forces. Most of them, especially those from the countryside, had never seen a weapon before. Within weeks, they were supposed to be transformed into soldiers and sent to the front.

My father was the only one who somehow maintained his composure. He stated that we were citizens of the country and had the duty to defend it whenever the necessity arose. Seated at the dinner table, he expressed his hope that the war wouldn't last long and that he would be back soon, with God's help.

On the last night, my mother packed his clothing and prepared a package of food. When dawn finally came, our house was full of people—my grandfather, his wife and her daughter, Manug Emmi's wife and children, my other grandparents' families, cousins and nephews. All had come to see my father off, and they bade him farewell with tearful embraces and mournful goodbyes. The other men from the other branches of our family eventually joined him at our house, and they all headed toward the recruitment office in the town square.

Every half-dozen or so steps, my father turned back and gazed longingly at us. My mother and other relatives cried hysterically and weakly waved their handkerchiefs in the air.

My father left that day, and we never saw him again.

We shared this fate with many households in town. We were not even told where our men had been taken. Nothing was ever heard of them.

⌣

The departure of our men began a chain of terrible events. It was as if our town had been struck by a curse. One evening, my grandfather returned home in a despondent state. He had heard the rumors circulating in the marketplace: supposedly, our town was now deemed an unsafe war zone, and the government was considering the evacuation of the population.

This policy was presented as an example of the government's magnanimity toward the Christian Armenian minority. We were to be moved south, for a few months at the most, to protect us from any military operations. This policy did not extend to Turks or Kurds, only to Armenians.

Some praised the Turks for their kind treatment of the Armenians during a time of war. They had not learned the lessons of the massacres and the persecution we had experienced over centuries of Ottoman rule. In the past, though, Armenians had never been exiled from their own lands. They had simply been targeted in their own homes and villages.

Almost every day, we received news that another town's Armenian population had been deported. We also heard isolated rumors of massacres and robberies that had been committed against them along the way. People's expressions hardened with fear and anxiety. The hitherto friendly relations between the Armenians and the Turks of our village crumbled. Now, neighbors of the two different nationalities couldn't even look each other straight in the eye.

One morning, a government crier appeared in the town square, accompanied by a small fat man who had a drum hanging from his neck. Occasionally, he struck the drum with a stick, drawing people's attention. At regular intervals, the crier repeated his message: all of the town's Armenians were to be moved to a safer area. The first caravan was set to leave in three days. The announcement spread across town like wildfire. The entire Armenian population was overtaken by shock and terror. Utter confusion reigned. People felt they had been smitten by God himself.

Government officials came around and announced: "Pack all that you can! It's war, folks, and the government has the duty to move you and protect you. God willing, you'll be returning home within two or three months. Don't be worried, the government has arranged for everything!"

We even heard them say to some of the neighbors: "Don't worry, leave your doors and windows open! When you return in a few months, everything will still be where you left it. The government pledges to protect your property and your belongings, just like it's protecting your lives!"

The people had no choice but to put their trust in these vapid words. Even those who knew better forced themselves to be optimistic.

My mother and grandmother were at their wits' end. They not only had just three days to pack our household for deportation, but also had to help my grandfather. Many valued items had to be left behind. We didn't have the ability to move large, extremely heavy items. The only beast of burden we owned was our donkey, and my grandfather didn't even have that. So, besides food and clothing, we packed only a few rugs and cushions, and we left the rest of the furniture behind. When we tied all the packages on the back of the donkey, the poor animal's knees buckled under the weight.

As the day of departure neared, the neighbors began assembling in our courtyard, speaking in ominous whispers. Where were they taking us? That was the chief question on everyone's mind. How would we live once we arrived at our destination? The caravans would be full of the elderly, women, and children. We couldn't fathom abandoning our homes, fields, animals, and the graves of our ancestors. Yet, we had to.

"Don't worry about what you leave behind!" repeated the crier. "We'll be here, guarding your properties and your homes. This is the government's pledge!"

My grandfather, as a respected elder, was very active, going everywhere, giving advice to everyone. He was one of the few healthy men left in the village, and his counsel was valued. The neighborhood women asked him to visit government officials in a nearby town and try to discover the fate that awaited us.

My grandfather acceded to their wishes. A few hours later, the women descended upon him before he had even properly entered the town.

"Hovhannes Emmi, what news do you have?" they all asked. "What did they say? What's going to happen to us? Where will we go? Will they really let us come back?"

Unfortunately, my grandfather had nothing new to say. The officials had told him what the crier had repeated for days: the evacuation was to ensure the safety of the Armenians. Everything had been meticulously planned and the Armenians would be protected by Turkish police and troops. One mullah had told my grandfather: "Brother, we have all lived on the same land, breathed the same air, and drank the same water. How can we entertain the idea of hurting our Armenian brethren?"

My grandfather could only repeat the same empty words. There was only one choice—to force oneself to believe the Turks' obvious lies, hoping against hope that they would honor their promises.

My mother worked without a single moment of rest. She prepared packages and our bags, chose which sheets, blankets, and rugs to take, decided which shoes we would wear. She packed bread, cheese, dried fruit, and hard-boiled eggs, but we had no idea how much of it to take.

We didn't have a carriage or a cart; all we had was the donkey. I was five years old, old enough to walk. I was told to hold the hands of my older cousins, Ardashes and Krikor, and walk with them beside the donkey.

The adults of the family spent our last night in Gurin in tears. Right before going to bed, my mother gave me some cheese and bread and ordered me to eat it for extra energy in the morning. After all, we didn't know how long we would be on the road.

Early the next morning, my grandfather came to our house and said that we would be leaving in a few moments. The policemen went house to house, asking people to leave their homes and join the departing caravan. My cousin Krikor helped my mother check that all packages were tied securely to the donkey. Then he helped her, my grandmother, and my siblings mount the poor animal and settle themselves amidst the baggage. We looked back, and for one last time we gazed at our open door, at our inviting courtyard, at the trees bordering our home, at the orchards and gardens beyond, at the mountains in the distance. Then, we all crossed ourselves. We were part of the first caravan leaving our town, and in its ranks were all the members of our extended family—almost forty households of the Panians, from octogenarians to suckling babies.

Only three policemen escorted us—one led the procession, while the other two proceeded on the flanks, keeping one eye on the rear of the line as well. They carried rifles.

Other families, too, had donkeys, mules, and even cows burdened with all kinds of baggage. We all kept looking back toward Gurin as it disappeared in the distance. We all seemed to be tortured by the same questions: Would we ever be back? Would we all survive to be reunited in our homes again? Were we abandoning our town to destruction?

A baby at the rear of the column burst into tears. Within seconds, other babies joined the chorus of wails.

The policemen stomped their feet, warning us not to slow down. I cast one last glance behind me. I could no longer see Gurin. All I could see were the peaks of those familiar mountains, which seemed to be bidding me a last, sad farewell.

We soon passed the village of Ghavakh. A few people quietly watched us go by. It was a village full of fields and orchards, but here, too, most of the doors were open, and the entire village seemed deserted. I wondered whether they had been made to leave like us.

As it passed noon, the sun beat down on us. My grandfather, despite leaning on his walking stick, led the caravan. Garo Emmi had one lame leg, but he walked quickly and with one of his grandchildren mounted on his shoulders. But some of the grandmothers were already having trouble walking. Most shuffled forward with their grandchildren holding their hands. Occasionally I heard them wailing in despair, "Dear God! When will this road end?"

We reached a dense thicket of trees. With the permission of our police escort, we stopped to rest. We put down our bags and bundles, and we lay down exhausted under the canopy of trees, trying to catch our breath.

Naturally, the policemen were tired, too, and they were hungry. They sat together in one corner of the woods and unpacked their bundles of food.

Following their example, each family gathered together and began eating. Some of the children, now rejuvenated, even started running around and playing together. At that moment, it almost looked like we were all out on a nature excursion instead of exiles from our homes. We still had the ability to play and have fun. If anything, we were more anxious than tired. The farther we got from our homes, the more perturbed our souls became. Among the adults, the exclusive topic of conversation under the trees was Gurin—their houses, their fields, their orchards, their cattle, their hens. They spoke nostalgically about the cold waters of the river, as if they had already been away from it for decades.

Nearby, under a tree, my grandfather was conversing with some other elderly men.

"This cursed war can't last more than ten or fifteen days," said Kevork Emmi.

"No, no, it'll last three to six months, I'm telling you," retorted Vartan Emmi. "It's ridiculous to speak of fifteen days. They wouldn't have made us leave if it were only going to last weeks. To be frank, I think this war will be much worse than we think."

"Why are we the only ones being evacuated?" complained Serop Emmi. "Why didn't they make the Turks leave, too? What difference does it make to the enemy if the people living in a certain town are Armenian or Turkish? If you ask me, whatever's going on, we Armenians are getting the short end of the stick."

The policemen ordered us to start moving again. Right behind the lead officer was my grandfather, who motioned to the rest of the people to follow. He was like a shepherd, guiding his people into strange lands. Few of us knew that my grandfather had actually been given a chance to save himself and his family from deportation. Turkish officials had told him that he would be allowed to stay in town when the others left, and thus save his own skin and the lives of his family members—including my mother, siblings, and me. He had categorically refused. He was Armenian to the core. Wherever his people went, that's where he would be found, alongside them. When the baffled officials had left him, he had told the women gathered around him, "They want me to stay here because they want to use me. They want me to build buildings for the government, houses for the rich Turks, roads and mosques. Then, one day, they'll force me to abandon my God and turn me into a Muslim. I'd rather die in the desert with my own people than live as a Judas while they're led to slaughter."

He had been granted his wish. He was with his people. There were other Armenians, too, whom the Turks had been ready to grant clemency, mostly skilled workers and important businessmen. None had decided to stay behind—the stigma of being branded as traitors was worse than any death.

The caravan continued its march toward the ever-distant horizon. It was a hot day, and the road was uneven, covered with sharp rocks. Some people were already falling by the wayside, exhausted, their laments filling the air. Still, we never stopped.

"This is just the beginning," said a woman.

"We'll see much worse, much worse," wailed another woman nearby, giving voice to her instincts.

The sun began setting, and the distant mountainsides faded into darkness. Would we cross those mountains? What would we find on the other side?

The policemen ordered us to stop for the night. Exhausted people collapsed onto the ground, thankful for finally being allowed to rest. Everyone still had plenty of food. My grandmother spread a sheet on the ground, and my mother neatly placed some of our food on it. We ate with relish, except for my sister, who fell asleep only after a few bites. My brother was exhausted, too, and soon dozed off. Though tired, I went to find my friends.

"Stay close to us! Don't play too rough!" called my mother after me.

The Armenian families huddled together, conversing in whispers. Many of the old men were chain-smoking under the trees. We little boys had energy to spare, and after a few minutes of running around we felt as comfortable as if we were playing in the fields of our own town.

It was late when I returned to my family. I found my brother and my sister calmly sleeping, as if they were back in their own beds. In their dreams, they probably were.

꒰

It had been three or four days since our departure. We had not been harassed along the way, and we didn't have much to complain of yet. We were made to walk four or five hours a day, but we were treated with decency. The policemen seemed to have no desire to mistreat us. We all hoped that these kind policemen would escort us all the way to our destination.

The terrible heat of the daytime had given way to a cool, clear night. The breeze blew through the branches and leaves of the trees, playing sweet melodies that reverberated through the air. For me, as a child, this was turning into quite an enjoyable excursion. I had no idea where we were, but we were surrounded by verdant valleys, and my friends and I couldn't ask for better playgrounds and a more pleasant journey.

We often came across travelers who politely greeted us, exchanged a few words, and then proceeded. I walked happily, holding on to my mother's hems. At every break, we sat and ate the usual bread and cheese, and I watched the adults gathered together, engaged in quiet conversation. At every break, my friends and I played to our heart's content.

That night, I slept well. In the morning, when I woke up, the people were already preparing to get back on the road. My mother and grand-mother were tying our bundles to our donkey. My grandfather, as usual, came by, embraced me, and kissed me. Then he walked over to the rest of the family, giving advice to my mother and grandmother as well as to the other families around us. Soon we heard a policeman's voice: "Let's try to hurry up today, and let's try to walk as far as we can before it gets very hot in the afternoon."

"How many more days will we be walking?" asked Garo Emmi.

"I don't know. We'll receive orders when necessary. Five or ten days, maybe."

This reply perturbed many of the Armenians. Another five or ten days? Some had thought they would be back home within that time frame.

"Yes, I think five or ten days," repeated the policeman. "But don't worry, we'll make sure you remain safe and sound."

A woman near the policeman raised her hands to the sky and whispered, "Lord, what have we done to deserve this?"

Five or ten more days. What choice did we have but to put our heads down and keep walking down the winding road? As the road grew worse, I began developing sores on the bottoms of my feet. I also saw more and more people falling by the wayside, and I heard wails of pain and exhaustion coming from the long column of marching humanity.

"Don't cry, my darling . . . Don't cry, my love . . . Just a little bit more walking . . . Come on, don't cry," said the mother of my friend Toros.

"You're a brave boy, don't worry, your wounds will heal, you'll feel better," said another mother to her son. Would the wounds really heal? Would things really get better? Would we ever recover the blood that was spilling onto the dirt and the grass?

In the last eight or ten hours we had taken only one break. We were praying for sunset, when we would be allowed to rest. None of us, men or women, old or young, had ever been so tired. Below our feet were pebbles and thorns, and in the distance we saw another chain of mountains, which undoubtedly we would cross. Sometimes we spotted hamlets or villages and sometimes we crossed fields, but we no longer saw other people. Did the fields belong to other Armenians, who had also been forcibly deported? These fields were ready to be harvested, their trees heavy with fruit, but there were no people in sight to enjoy this bounty of nature.

In the sky was the pitiless sun, beating down on us. Not a single body of water was to be seen anywhere. Sweat ran down our brows and our cheeks, dripping onto the ground.

"Water! Water!" came the cries from everywhere.

"We'll be there soon! Not much walking left!" announced one of the policemen.

The elderly faltered and stumbled to the ground, tormented by exhaustion and thirst. "Leave me! You keep going! I can't get up," I heard a grandmother say to her family while her young sons, daughters-in-law, and grandchildren gathered around her, sobbing uncontrollably. The policemen reached her. "Come on, lady, come on, stand up. We'll soon get to water, stand up."

We didn't know whether the policemen were telling the truth or whether they were simply trying to keep us walking. They were guiding the caravan in a southern direction, according to orders they had received.

The following day, we still had not seen water and the heat had become even more stifling. Our mental and physical strength kept eroding, like a rock exposed to the elements. Despite the pervading misery, some of the older men took it upon themselves to enhearten the rest. My grandfather, leaning on his walking stick, ran up and down the caravan, exhorting everyone to keep marching: "Remember! Our Lord Jesus Christ himself had to carry his cross, had to face his Calvary! We, too, are Christians. We must remember our savior and tolerate our suffering with dignity, like he did!"

There was something prophetic in these words. Yes, we were all Christians, and it seemed that just like our savior we would die on a cross.

"To suffer is the fate of all Christians—to surrender is not!" he said. "All of this will come to an end! Our forefathers had to walk this thorny road, too. It's now our turn, and it's our duty to keep marching, to keep going, to reach the end and to survive!"

On the eighth day of marching, those up front spotted a stream in the distance.

"Water! Water!" came the cry from ahead. Soon a stampede began. As if overtaken by collective hysteria, almost every man, woman, and child jumped into the water. We drank to our hearts' content, and we washed ourselves for the first time in more than a week. Everyone forgot their exhaustion and misery.

The animals were unpacked. We were to spend the night here, on the banks of the stream.

"Sleep well, and try to get as much rest as you can. Didn't we tell you we'd get to water soon?" spoke one of the policemen, smiling contentedly.

We all seemed to have forgotten the suffering and thirst of the past few days. Once again, we were lying in a verdant meadow, on lush grass, beside a gurgling stream. We had food and water, and the night was cool and breezy. For the moment, we were content.

As they had done before, the families gathered together and opened their bundles of food. The bread, cheese, boiled eggs, and dried fruit that my mother had packed for the journey had lasted all this time, and there was still a decent portion left. We had been allowed to eat only twice a day, after all.

The infants and young children were bundled in blankets and slept peacefully on the soft grass. The women's conversations returned to the fate of their children. Most of these women had never attended school themselves, but almost all of them believed fervently in the power of education. Since the closure of our own town's school, the desire to see their children educated had become almost a fixation with these women. Now that we were being deported, their concern for education turned into a true obsession. These unfortunate women, having lost their husbands, had to care for their children under impossible circumstances. As I went to sleep that night, I heard them speak of the fields they had left behind.

"Don't worry about our crops. I'm sure the Turks have already either stolen or burned everything," stated Vartuhi Khanum,[*] with her gallows humor.

"Before our caravan even left town, ten or twenty Turks showed up at

---

[*] *Khanum* is a Turkish-language honorific for respected married women.

our orchards. They stole whatever they could, then trampled and destroyed the rest," added another woman.

"This is exile, I tell you, exile! They'll drive us away, and we'll never be allowed to return home! The Turks have just been waiting for this day so they can rob us of everything we have and kill us all!" wailed a grandmother, her voice shaking with rage.

"She's right. They are exiling us from our ancestors' lands. We've fallen into hellfire and we won't get out of it until we've burned to ashes!" agreed Surpig Khanum.

"You see the worst in everything. You're scaring us all," reprimanded Nektar Khanum from her corner.

Nearby, the old men were expressing their views on the ongoing Great War, on the battles that had been fought. Some predicted the outcome of the hostilities and picked the victors. A strange phenomenon—the women spoke of their homes and families, while the men discussed global, universal, and impersonal issues.

We walked on. Already our shoes had holes in them, our clothing was in tatters, and a layer of gray dust had made us unrecognizable to each other. More important, our very souls were undergoing a monumental transformation. Young brides had aged by decades, and the children looked like feral beasts, their eyes gleaming wildly.

It had only been eight or ten days since we had left our town. Like all the other kids, I had already bidden farewell to the innocence of my childhood. I was a small boy, yet the misery I was witnessing was already teaching me the bitter, cynical lessons that most people learn only after a lifetime of suffering.

We spent another night in the open, near the stream we had been following, and we slept on the grass, which wasn't so bad. After our meal, I huddled up next to my mother, leaned back against the stump of a tree, and surrendered to my reflections. My shoes would not survive another day of marching—the soles were coming undone. I knew I would have to walk barefoot within a day or two. I had spent my entire life in prosperity, always having been blessed with plenty. Would I now survive? I asked myself that question, and, strangely, a voice within me answered right away—yes, I would. I had a strange, firm belief in the certainty of my own survival.

This inner voice was very powerful and confident. I could see ants crawling in the grass, I could hear crickets near the stream, and above me birds flew to and from their nests, feeding their chicks. Seeing all of this inspired me with strength and determination. I had an intense desire to go on living.

I had come this far, and I would keep walking as long as I had to. At this moment, I remembered the Lord's Prayer, which my mother had taught me. "And lead us not into temptation, but deliver us from evil," I repeated silently, without even understanding the words. All I knew was that a strange confidence grew within me every time I repeated the phrase, as if God himself were whispering me words of encouragement.

"Eat your bread, dear, you'll need your strength," said my mother.

"Do we still have lots of bread, mother?" I asked.

"We have enough for now . . . Don't worry, dear," she replied solemnly.

As usual, I made the sign of the cross and then chewed down my bread. That's all we had to eat that day. We had already finished our eggs and our cheese.

I thought of the beggars who had occasionally knocked on our door and asked for bread. We would give them a few old scraps, and they would leave after showering us with blessings. Would we share those poor people's fate soon? Yet I knew that we had some money. Both my mother and my grandmother had sewn coins into their belts and clothing. We would not be completely destitute. I clung to this idea with desperation, consoling myself that we were still wealthy. We just needed to get to a town where that money could be put to use.

One day, slightly past noon, we came across the relatively large town of Elbistan. Surrounded by woodlands, it was, from first sight, easily discernible as a wealthy city. We didn't enter the city itself, but as we went around it some curious onlookers came to watch our sad procession. A few had brought freshly baked loaves of bread in baskets, which were all very quickly purchased. My grandfather bought some for our family—we devoured those circular, fragrant loaves.

However, we couldn't eat to our heart's content. For the first time in my life, I was introduced to the concept of rationing. My mother divided the bread into equal pieces and gave us each our share. I ate my portion and looked up at her, wanting to ask for more. She preempted me.

"That's enough for today, we'll save the rest for tomorrow," she said curtly. Something about her voice, and something about the expression in her eyes, ripped my soul apart. At that moment I understood that the menace of hunger hung over us. From then on, we would have only dry bread, and not enough of it.

After marching for about ten days, we heard that we were near Marash.* Many in the caravan had visited this city, which seemed like a metropolis, before. As in Elbistan, we never entered the city proper but went around it, and again many merchants were waiting for us on the side of the road. This time, they had not only bread, but also tomatoes, cucumbers, and other vegetables. The caravan came to a halt. As the adults made their purchases, they engaged the locals in conversation. We discovered that the Armenians of Marash had not been deported yet, but they feared it would come soon.

The merchants refused to accept money. The Armenian Prelacy had paid them already, and they distributed the food freely to all, receiving our gratitude and our blessings. Some were Armenian, and they wished us the best with tears in their eyes: "You've gotten this far safe and sound, may God watch over you for the rest of the way."

"And we hope they'll let you stay in your homes. We hope you won't share our fate," replied some of the old men among us. Then the caravan had to move on.

We now had enough food to last another few days. As we left Marash, our poor donkey could barely keep up with us. My mother and my grandmother alternated riding on its back, each with either my little sister or brother. I was never offered a place on the donkey's back. I didn't complain, since my younger siblings would have had much more trouble walking. I

---

* Marash is now known as Kahramanmaraş.

followed the donkey on foot, playing with my friends along the way whenever I was able to forget my thirst and exhaustion.

Even when I was tired and could barely keep up, I didn't want to show it.
My mother would grab my hand and exhort me to keep going, to keep pace.
Other children my age also went on foot, and I didn't want to lose face by
asking the women and infants of my family to yield their place on the back
of the donkey to me.

My grandfather would often come to us and speak to my mother and
grandmother. He would then flash his eternal smile and kiss me. He would
do the same with the other children of our family, and even with the children of friends and neighbors. He had enough love to share with all of the
boys and girls. Many thought that the reason we had not been attacked and
robbed was because of the respect he commanded from the Turks. When
he spoke to the policemen, they stood at attention, saluted him, and replied
politely, as if addressing a superior officer. When anybody fell to the ground
exhausted during the marches, he was often the first to rush to them. Despite
his advanced age, he was one of the healthiest men among us. He was quick,
observant, and willing to help anyone. As he walked, he prayed. His name
was never absent from the prayers and blessings of the others in the caravan.

I never witnessed anybody display so much grace under such terrible
circumstances. Every morning, my grandfather woke up, crossed himself,
and began his prayers with his usual, "Lord, I beseech you to bless and protect my family." Strengthened by his communion with God, he began his
day with exuberance. He was more pious than even the town's clergy, and
he truly believed in the power of his prayers.

"Hovhannes Emmi, when will this cursed march end?" asked an anxious
woman.

"Only God knows," he replied. "Even the policemen don't know for
sure. But one of these days we're bound to reach our destination."

"We've already been walking for a fortnight," bemoaned another woman.

We walked like a flock of sheep, obedient and submissive, tormented by
our memories and our fears, but unwilling to speak up. We had not been
attacked. We hadn't even been physically threatened. But by this point

everyone in the caravan sensed that this forced march would end in death. Most were already resigned to this reality, and with that realization came apathy. What could we do?

We kept walking. The never-ending road wound its way through the land. We spotted mountains blocking our way, and we crossed them, only to face new mountains, new hills, and new fields. Every day was hotter than the preceding one, and often the ground burned our feet through the soles of our shoes.

"I can't walk anymore!" cried out a lady, and she fell to the ground. People rushed to her, begging her to get back to her feet.

"Go on without me! Just leave me here to die," pitifully murmured the poor woman. "I can't bear this anymore, I can't bear it! I want to die!"

"We won't leave you behind! Come on! Get back to your feet! God will keep watch over you!"

She was one of the women of our town who had lost a son to the general mobilization. Her grief had turned to despair, and she had now given up, no longer even thinking of her other children. She simply wanted to die to be free of all this. She had been walking non-stop for two weeks, told that our destination was just around the next bend, and promised that she would soon be back home. Now that she finally saw through the Turks' lies, she could not go on living. She had lost all hope.

༄

"Tomorrow we'll be in Aintab,"* said one of the policemen, as we spent another night in the open.

"Is Aintab our destination?" everyone asked hopefully.

"God willing, yes. And we'll then leave you, as well," replied the policeman.

"Where will we live? Will they give us homes? Will we see our husbands there?" asked some of the women.

"Don't fret, they've arranged for everything."

---

* Aintab was a major city in the Ottoman province of Aleppo. It was home to a large and prosperous Armenian community involved in trade and agriculture.

"Who? Who's going to take care of us? We don't even have our men," insisted the women, their voices shaking with doubt.

"Don't worry, the government will look after you."

"And will you stay with us?" naively asked an elderly lady.

"Our job was to escort you to Aintab. Once we get you to the city, we'll return to Gurin."

That evening, after more than two weeks of forced marches, we spotted Aintab in the distance, perched at the feet of mountains, in a wide valley. Through the trees we could already distinguish the roofs of houses.

"We're here! We're in Aintab!" The caravan instinctively sped its pace. We reached a large field on the outskirts of town, where we spent the night before going into the city proper the next day. Many slept well that night.

Soon, several Armenians came out to us from the city, bringing with them bread, rice pilaf, and plenty of the salty yoghurt drink called *tan*. This was the first proper, fresh meal we'd had for weeks.

The elderly men talked to the locals, describing to them the privations that the caravan had suffered in the past few weeks. The fact that the Aintab Armenians had not been deported helped persuade us that the city would be our last stop and we would be settled here.

As night fell, we children forgot our exhaustion. Fueled by the food, we started running around the field and playing our games. The old men watched us and smiled, our games lifting their spirits.

"We used to play these same games, too, when we were children," mused Kevork Emmi.

"Who do you think taught them these games?" replied Vartan Emmi.

At one point, while running about, I looked back and saw my mother sitting under a tree, with my brother and my sister on her lap. As she watched me play, she seemed to be deep in thought, though I have no idea what she was thinking. She looked utterly spent. She had aged greatly in the past few weeks. Her eyes were void of their usual gleam. She suffered not only for herself, but also for us.

Suddenly, there were cries of joy from the crowd—an Armenian priest was heading toward us, alongside a few other men who seemed to be important officials from Aintab. They talked to the old men, discussed what had happened since the caravan had left Gurin, and prayed with us before returning to the city.

Tired from my games, I lay my head down on my mother's knees and watched the sky above. I listened to the soft whispers of the leaves and watched the stars wink blue and yellow from high above. At some point, I must have drifted into sleep. I don't know how long it had been, but suddenly I was awoken by cries from all around me: "Thieves! Thieves! We've been robbed!"

"What are they talking about? Thieves? Would thieves really attack our miserable caravan?" mumbled Vartan Emmi beside me.

"How many of them were there?" called out Garbo Emmi. There was no reply. Nobody knew. But clearly, the caravan had been robbed. They had stolen a large vat and a rug from one family.

"Idiots! They must have fallen on hard times. Couldn't they find a better target than a bunch of miserable deportees?" lamented my grandfather.

The criminals had disappeared into the night, but now everyone in the caravan was wide awake. Men and women gathered in their small groups to discuss the event. The thieves could not have been Armenian, many argued. They must have been Turks.

"They're all thieves! Their entire race! Besides, no Armenian would do such a terrible thing!" pontificated an old man.

As the day dawned, most stopped talking about the theft, and turning eastward, began praying. They sang the *Aravod Louso*,* addressing the rising sun, their eyes turned upward. God was now the only thing they could rely on, the only power that could rescue them. The solid faith of these suffering exiles may have seemed naive, but to them it was the only solid thing in their universe, and they truly believed that God would come to their aid. Kind hearts are often filled with such unworldly faith.

Already there was a decent amount of traffic going in and out of the city. A few men and women approached us, again bearing gifts of bread, cheese,

---

* "Morning of Light," a poem/hymn by Nerses Shnorhali (Nerses the Gracious), Catholicos of Armenia from 1166 to 1173.

and yogurt. Each family received a few days' supply of food. The locals and the exiles chatted like old acquaintances, and, unfortunately, during these early morning conversations, the locals expressed their fears that we might not, after all, settle in Aintab. They had already seen several caravans halt at the city, only to then continue their way toward the Syrian desert.

"Is that desert far from here? How many days' walk is it?"

"We're speaking of the desert in northern Syria, in the areas of Deir al-Zor, Qamishli, Meskene, Hama and Homs, all the way to the Hauran in southern Syria," answered one of the locals.

"From here, it's a few hours to the town of Kilis, and from Kilis a few hours' walk until the desert begins."

In my mind, the borders of the known world had always been the mountains and valleys that surrounded Gurin. In the past two weeks, as I had marched alongside the others, these borders had greatly expanded. Now that I had reached Aintab, I was learning that there were still other cities and towns, and even these things called a desert—a vast area full of sand and dirt, extremely hot and arid, where people did not live.

We were baffled. Our doubts grew, and we didn't know whom to believe. In our despair, we looked into each other's eyes, seeing nothing but our own terror reflected in the gaze of others. In our understanding, going into the desert was tantamount to a sentence of death—and a slow one.

My grandfather had fallen silent. He was leaning against a tree, lost in his thoughts, occasionally shaking his head. "We've marched all the way here in relative safety, but now . . ." he murmured, still lost in his meditations. Even he, who was always known for his unshakeable optimism, had begun to doubt.

We spotted some policemen coming toward us from the city. They were set to replace our escorts, with whom they were now conversing intently in a corner. A few minutes later, the kind policemen who had come all the way with us from Gurin wished us a safe journey and turned back toward our town.

"Gather your belongings! We'll be leaving momentarily!" called out one of the new policemen in an authoritative voice.

There was nothing to gather. Everything was ready. We had become accustomed to packing and unpacking quickly. We formed a line, at the head of which were the donkeys and oxen, with their riders, followed by the masses on foot.

We followed the policemen around the city without a murmur or a complaint, and we soon left Aintab behind. Within minutes we could no longer see the city behind us. It had disappeared behind a sharp bend in the road. We marched in complete silence, dejected and downcast, but unable or unwilling to even complain, like obedient animals being marched to the slaughterhouse.

CHAPTER 3

THE DESERT

WITH EVERY PASSING MOMENT we put more distance between our-selves and Gurin, as well as between ourselves and any civilized life. My mind traveled back to our house, to my warm bed, to our fields and trees, to the bread we used to bake in our tonir. All of it was gone, though at the time I could not entertain the possibility that I would never again set foot in Gurin.

The sun was hotter now. I began suffering from intense thirst. It seemed as if I was being baked from the inside. Along the road, the leaves and weeds were desiccated, and in some places the ground had cracks running through it.

As the sun set, we spotted the outlines of Kilis in the middle distance. We could see men working in the fields right outside the city's walls.

We stayed in a large field of wheat outside of the city. Again, we were not allowed to enter the city proper. None of us could sleep. Many people in our group crushed grains of wheat in their hands and ate them, trying to get some sustenance. The unripe grains tasted strange, like sour milk.

"If only we had a fire, we could cook the grains and eat them. They'd taste marvelous," wished Vartan Emmi.

"We used to do that back in our fields, but this isn't our wheat. What right do we have to steal?" interjected Garbo Emmi. "Oh, how things have changed, and how quickly! We used to eat, drink, and smoke to our heart's content. The world's been turned upside down, I tell you."

In the morning, the usual scene was repeated: Armenians from the city came out to us, bringing bread with them. Each family received a few loaves. These people would not look us in the eye and seemed to be on the verge of tears. They told us that several other caravans had passed through Kilis recently, but most had been in a terrible state. They had been ambushed along the route and robbed of their belongings, and there had even been several kidnappings. They were very worried that they, too, would soon be deported.

We marched on, covered in layers of dirt. Sometimes, when the road bordered fields, men would look up from their work and wish us a happy journey, unaware of what was happening. Some even offered us fruit from their gardens. We took the fruit, thanked them, and moved on.

Unlike the policemen who had accompanied us from Gurin to Aintab, the new guards gave their orders harshly, and they seemed capable of much worse. "Why are you slowing down? Come on! Forward!" they yelled.

They didn't think of the elderly and the children, and they didn't entertain the possibility that some of the weaker members of the caravan could not possibly walk any faster. When the sun reached its zenith in the sky, its rays cooked us alive. The thirst was becoming unbearable.

We kept going, with gritted teeth, because we had no choice. We marched on, whipped forward by the remonstrations of the policemen.

"When will this end? Three weeks have gone by, and we keep going," whispered Vartanush Mayrig.*

"Don't think of it, just keep walking. It can't go on forever. This too, shall pass," said my grandfather.

"We can't go on forever, either! We'll all die soon! Isn't that what they want?" exclaimed a mother carrying her exhausted child in her arms, barely keeping up with the rest of us.

Almost everyone in the caravan had fallen into despair. Men and women, old and young, they all saw only darkness. These people, who just weeks earlier had been prosperous, living in their homes, praying in their churches,

---

* *Mayrig* literally means "mother," but could be used as a term of respect for older women—relatives or strangers—as well as for female caretakers in schools and orphanages.

working in their fields, and helping the less fortunate, had been turned into a race of emaciated semi-corpses. They were like plants that had been uprooted and cast aside, and they were now dying slowly, shriveling into nothing.

In the far distance, the dying rays of the setting sun lit up the mountain peaks. We were slowly heading in that direction, and I knew that the desert would begin after we crossed them. "Mother, have you ever seen this desert?" I asked.

"No, my son, I've only heard about deserts in fairy tales. They're supposed to be like endless fields of sand and dirt, where it's very hot all the time."

I heard other descriptions of the desert, too, and I was filled with horror at the idea of being lost in it. I imagined an entire world of burning sand and nothing else—each grain of sand a spark of fire. It would be impossible to walk on that sand, especially in shoes without soles. What would we drink? What would we eat?

That evening, the caravan reached the outskirts of a town, where we stopped near some metallic tracks that ran parallel to each other. Nearby were two buildings blackened with smoke and soot. We were told to unpack our animals here. I looked at my sister and brother—both were exhausted and extremely sleepy. One can imagine what state I was in. I wasn't that much older than they were, and unlike them, I had spent the past three weeks walking rather than riding the donkey.

From behind the nearest hill, we heard a shrill, ear-piercing whistle that seemed to be coming closer. The whistle ceased, then started again, until, around the bend, we saw a huge machine, belching smoke and steam, dragging compartments behind it. The machine screeched to a halt in front of the blackened building.

"It's a train!" yelled Vartan Emmi excitedly.

"Train? What's a train?" asked others.

Most of the people in the caravan had never even heard the word.

"Do you see that huge chimney? It's a machine that uses the power of steam to move. Those are the wagons, and the compartment in the front is called a locomotive. It transports goods and people from place to place. I think we'll soon be riding it toward the desert."

Fear gripped my heart. My imagination was running amok. Huddled behind my mother, I gawked at the terrifying steam machine. I would have preferred walking for another three weeks, or three months, rather than be forced to enter that dreadful contraption.

The doors of the wagons were pulled open. Soldiers and civilians alighted from them, and soon people were yelling, calling to each other, haggling. Many locals were there, trying to sell fruit and other local products.

Many of us in the caravan took this chance to buy more food. Soon, we were all made to gather near the train. Eyeing it with doubt and fear, we waited for further orders.

One of the policemen, ominously swinging a whip in one hand, told us to board the wagons. Four or five wagons were enough for all the members of the caravan. We stayed together. My grandfather's family, Manug Emmi's family, ours, my uncle and his wife, and the families of Garbo, Kevork, and Vartan Emmis all crammed into one wagon. Two soldiers guarded us, their rifles at the ready. The donkeys, mules, and oxen remained outside, staring at us in dazed stupor.

Our donkey had served us obediently for so many years, without ever complaining, even when forced to bear excessive weight, such as he had during our deportation. Now it was being taken away. Some people asked what would happen to the animals.

"We put you on a comfortable train, now you want us to spend money transporting your animals, too?" indignantly replied one of the soldiers. He continued: "They'll be sent after you on the next train. Don't worry, the government will make sure they get to where you're going."

Obviously, it was pointless to argue.

We heard three more blasts of that shrill whistle, and then a low rumbling as we felt the wagons moving. At first we advanced slowly, but within minutes the train was slicing through the air like a young colt. We whimpered in the belly of this hellish machine, racing to our next destination.

The silence of the night was disturbed only by the sounds of the wheels and the engine. Exhausted and terrified, I put my head down on my mother's knee and tried to sleep, but I couldn't.

My grandmother took my hand and squeezed a piece of bread into it. "Eat it, my dear," she said. "Before you go to sleep, eat some bread." She didn't know when we would be able to eat again.

We were all facing the prospect of starvation in the desert. Death was a common feature in everybody's conversations, as if we collectively felt the angel of death looming above us.

The train made a few stops during the night, but each time it only halted for a few minutes before continuing its mad gallop through the darkness. There were no lights in the countryside along the tracks. Through the small window all I could see was a patch of sky and stars flitting across it.

As the sun rose on the horizon and silhouettes appeared in the dark, we noticed small shacks on the side of the tracks. We spotted the city of Hama. It was squeezed between two rivers, just like our Gurin.

The train screeched to a halt, and we were ordered off the wagons. As soon as we left the train station, I realized that we were now in the desert. But I didn't see sand. The entire area outside the station was flooded with a sea of humanity. It was full of Armenians who had been deported from their own regions and had arrived before us.

All across the sand and dirt, in the open air, without even a tree to offer shade, were masses of huddled women and children. Here was our last destination. I could see the other bank of the river—green, verdant, buzzing with life. But on this side of the water, there was nothing.

I gazed around me, and I finally understood exactly what the desert was—not a single standing structure, not even a tent. Here and there, people had improvised shelter by putting together hovels made of their clothing, but those offered scant protection against the sun and the heat. Our caravan settled into an unoccupied corner. Our neighbors were Armenians from different parts of Sepastia and Cilicia.* There were probably twenty or thirty thousand exiles just from those areas. Each community tended to

---

* Sepastia (now known as Sivas) is an area in central Anatolia. Cilicia is a region along the southeastern coast of modern Turkey that also encompassed parts of northern Syria. Home to the Kingdom of Cilician Armenia from 1080 to 1375 and then under the dominion of the Ottoman Empire from the fifteenth century until the end of World War I, Cilicia was to become an independent Armenian state, but instead it was made part of Turkey.

stick together; the Armenians of Sepastia, of Zeytun,[*] of Malatya, each had their own "neighborhood" in the camp. Our lot was right beside those from Sepastia.

We spent the first few days in this desert outside Hama simply coming to grips with the fate that had befallen us. We were surrounded by Armenians from all parts of the Ottoman Empire, speaking dozens of different dialects. Some had different customs and dress, too, but two things united us—we all were Armenian Christians, and we had all been deported from our homes and ancestral lands.

"There were three thousand people in our caravan," said an older man from among the Sepastia exiles. "It was hell. We were ambushed, killed, robbed. So many couldn't walk, couldn't even stand on their own feet anymore. Many died along the way, and some were kidnapped. Only a few hundred of us made it here alive."

"The Arapkır and Malatya caravans were merged together, and when they reached the Syrian border they were attacked by brigands carrying rifles, swords, and axes," related an old man who had, by some miracle, escaped. "They killed the old men and women, and they kidnapped the young girls. I saw them impaling babies with their swords, then waving them in the air before smashing them against the ground. Most of the people in the caravan were massacred. The few who survived ran to the nearby mountains."

The population of the camp grew every day. The newcomers were all Armenians. That was their only crime. They had been gathered from all over the country, brought here to die in the sands of the desert.

Every new day was another apocalyptic vision. The sun and the heat were ruthless enemies, and there was not nearly enough food, clean water, or medication for the swelling population of deportees. Soon, diseases like cholera and typhus became endemic throughout the camp. Children and infants made up the majority of those who succumbed to illness. They usually died in terrible pain.

Despite the gruesome conditions, some of the women had organized

---

[*] Zeytun is now Süleymanlı.

small groups that tried to help sick people and pregnant women. The number of deaths far outweighed the number of births.

For every sick person who was miraculously healed, five to ten died.
Hunger, thirst, and the unbearable heat transformed the sick into ghostly,
terrifying skeletons.

There were neither fences nor barbed wire surrounding the camp, but
we were under strict orders never to leave the desert or to enter the city.
We were restricted to a tiny area where we slowly fried to death under the
searing sun.

My sister was already weak. She spent her days in my mother's lap, and
once in a while she would open her parched lips and whisper in a barely
audible voice, "Water, Mama, water."

There was no water, and my mother was running out of her small supply
of medicine. She constantly sang lullabies to my sister and kept her in bed,
so that she would sleep and at least forget her thirst for most of the day.

After sunset, the air got a little cooler. At these times, some locals came
to the camp with bread and large cauldrons of pilaf. "If you catch cholera,
you'll take those germs back to the city with you and start an epidemic!"
warned the policemen. But such threats did not stifle the humanitarian
instincts of these good people.

Unfortunately, though, this generous assistance mutated into commer-
cial opportunism. In time, bread and fruit were no longer free. The supply
was insufficient and the demand was huge, leading to exorbitant prices.

Soon, water ceased to be free, too. The merchants took full advantage
of our misery. They quadrupled their prices from one day to the next, and
still the deportees would trample each other to buy the last of the supplies.
They knew they were being exploited, but what could they do? This was an
existential struggle.

☙

My mother became withdrawn and taciturn. Still, she always took care to
split every loaf of bread into four equal pieces for us. It was dry bread, and
there was nothing else. At nights, the pangs of hunger kept me up. I would

stay awake and in my mind fly back home, recalling the orchards and their fruit, the stream's frigid waters, the picnics in the meadows.

We were still alive, but we were surrounded by the entire gamut of human suffering, unable to do anything to help us and those around us. "He's gone! My boy is dead!" screamed a woman from nearby, plucking her hair out with her emaciated fingers. "How can I go on living? Whom should I live for now?"

The other women gathered around her, trying vainly to console her. How could they? Each was suffering. Each had her own burden to bear.

Some among these women never complained, never cursed their luck. Their fate was unshakeable, and they bore their cross without a whimper, with utmost dignity and strength. "We'll keep praying for God's aid until there's no one left alive to pray anymore," said one woman.

We started hearing of kidnappings in the camp. Despite the terrible conditions, some young girls had preserved their beauty, and local men paid visits to these girls' mothers, bringing food and delicacies, promising to get their families out of the camp if they agreed to allow their daughters to marry them. Every single one of these proposals was rejected. Some of the spurned suitors, with the assistance and support of the soldiers guarding the camp, kidnapped these girls with brute force. Most of the victims were very young, no more than thirteen or fourteen years old, while their captors were in their thirties or forties.

One especially corpulent, dirty man was over the age of fifty. He was taken with a specific girl, very beautiful, and had been chasing her around the camp for some time. He eventually presented himself to her parents, bearing a gift of baked goods and sweets on a large silver tray. The parents refused his advances and sent their daughter to stay with some relatives elsewhere in the camp. They were hungry and suffering, and they could have greatly improved their lot had they agreed, but they refused to tarnish their family's honor and forsake their daughter. The suitor had even bribed the guards to intercede on his behalf with the girl's parents. "Just let him have her!" they advised. "She'll be in a safe place, and you'll be saved, too." But the parents would not budge. Their decision was final.

When another pretty girl fell victim to disease, her mother said, "God took her soul so she wouldn't have to lie with the Arab." She couldn't even cry any longer.

～

More than a hundred and twenty people from my extended family had reached the camp; none of us had come to any harm along the way. Other groups had been attacked, robbed, raped, and killed, and only a small fraction of those who had left their homes had arrived at the camp in Hama.

All twenty-two Panian families at the camp tried their best to survive. We looked upon my grandfather, the central authority of the clan, as our guardian angel. Sometimes he inspired us to feel optimistic about our prospects. "We'll be back, don't worry, we'll soon be back home," he would say, as if he was interpreting a dream. Our hope occasionally lulled us into a false sense of comfort.

Yet we were surrounded by death and misery. A cart made the rounds around the camp, collecting dead bodies. At first it made two trips per day— one at noon, one at night—but now it made five or six tours of the camp just to catch up with the rising death toll.

The desert seemed intent on destroying every vestige of life. From the camp, we could see the city and the river running by it, and we could hear the wheels of the large water mill turning. There, even the trees had enough water to drink. Just a few miles away, we were dying of thirst.

In the evenings, when the wind blew south, the stench of the bodies filled the air. It was nauseatingly sweet. This fetid air must have been one reason for the diseases running rampant through the camp. Sometimes people didn't even know they were sick, until one day they keeled over, burned up in fevers, and suffered from terrible pains before dying. Most such casualties, by this point, were children, but adults fell like flies, too, taking their last breath with maledictions and curses. The camp was basically turning into a large graveyard. People stopped even keeping tally of the dead. People simply died, and none of us could spare the time or effort to care about them personally.

Two weeks after reaching Hama, my family's numbers began dwindling, too. Two small children, distant relatives of mine, were the first to die. They were put on the cart and were taken away, followed by a few women who wailed and cried the entire way. They were buried in a nearby ditch.

"Without any prayers, without a priest. They were just thrown into a hole and left there," bemoaned Marta Abla.*

"We couldn't even look down into the ditch. There were other bodies in there, and the stench was unbearable. They were just thrown in," added Takuhi Khanum.

"At least they'll never become orphans," said Kevork Emmi, sounding almost coldhearted. In a way, though, he was right. What would have become of those two infants had they survived their mother and grandparents? They would have been alone in the world.

Two days after the passing of the two children, my grandfather's wife and daughter both died, one after the other. My grandfather was now alone. He began spending all of his time with us, and we now split every loaf of bread into five, instead of four.

My cousin Krikor was one of the healthiest and strongest boys in the family. Thus, he was tasked with trying his best to finagle whatever bread he could from the merchants who came down the road from the city. My grandfather gave Krikor a yellow round coin every morning. Krikor would often get bread after haggling for lower prices, so that he could bring back smaller metallic coins to my grandfather, who would stroke his hair and bless him. "Good work, my son. You could get bread from stones."

Krikor woke up early every morning and went to his usual spot, crowded by others, and sometimes stood there for hours before getting bread. As the number of deportees grew, it became almost impossible to supply them all with bread. There were often tussles and even fights over it. Many, like Krikor, were procuring food for entire extended families.

Every few days, the price rose. The buyers paid the higher prices without complaints. What choice did they have?

---

* *Abla* means "aunt" in Turkish.

One day, Krikor returned empty-handed and injured. The people who had gathered to buy bread had started fighting, and Krikor had been struck a few times in the face, leaving him with a bloody nose. All of us spent that day hungry. We didn't have any water, either. It was a situation we were becoming accustomed to. The next day, my aunt turned to Krikor and said: "My son, go get us some bread. This time, stay close to the guards. They won't let anyone raise a hand against you."

My grandfather then handed Krikor one of the yellow coins and added: "Buy as much as you can find. Don't bring back any money; just bring as much bread as you can carry."

Krikor took the money and left. We gazed after him, full of admiration. He was our hero. He was responsible for keeping us alive, and no matter what the risk, he never shrunk from the duty. On his way, he was joined by some other boys his age who were the breadwinners of their own families.

Hours passed, and Krikor didn't reappear. We became very restless and worried. "He's late. I'm going to go look for him and find out what happened," said my aunt, her voice shaking with anxiety. She entrusted her youngest, Ardashes, to my mother's care, and walked away.

After a long wait, Krikor finally returned with his mother. He was sweating profusely, but the full bag on his back was proof that his adventures had not been in vain. The bread sellers had come late, and they had once again demanded exorbitant prices. Thankfully, some of the guards had intervened and forced the merchants to sell the bread at a reasonable price.

I was accustomed to eating bread with butter, jam, or cheese, but now I ate it dry with ravenous relish. Hunger, after all, is the best spice. Every time I bit into those crusty loaves, I thanked and praised God for such bounty. I wanted to live.

In those days, families that still had money could survive in the camp. The majority of the exiles, however, had been robbed during their long march, which meant they were condemned to beg for scraps to keep body and soul intact. Every day, hundreds of these unfortunates took their last breath in the desert inferno.

One day, while wandering around the camp, I found my old friends

Sahag and Garo, whom I had not heard from since arriving at Hama. Their families were staying on the other side of the camp. They said they had been looking for me and finally found me. During those terrible days, just seeing each other alive was a source of great joy for all three of us. But how they had changed! Their eyes were no longer brilliant, their feet were unshod, their clothes were in tatters, and their long hair covered most of their face.

We sat on the sand and chatted, but not about the old days, or about the games we used to play. All of that was in the past and was probably no longer possible in the future. Now we were in a grim place, surrounded by pestilence and hunger, pain and death. We talked about food and death.

"Have you folks been finding bread?" asked Sahag.

"Has anyone in your family died yet?" asked Garo.

We talked for a while, but then it got quiet. We stared at each other, looking deep into each other's eyes, yet no words came to our lips. I think all three of us were lost in reminiscences of our old town, of how we used to play with such abandon, how we used to eat and drink gluttonously. Had anyone ever told us that we'd go hungry, we would have laughed in their face.

Soon Sahag and Garo went back to their side of the camp. I was left alone, lost in my reveries.

That evening, my mother decided that we needed some "fresh air," so she took us out of the camp and into the desert. The poor woman was trying her best to get her children away from that hellish place, even if for only a few hours. But what good could it do when we were so parched? We wanted water and not much else.

When the sun set, we went back to our usual corner of the camp. My grandmother had stayed behind to guard our possessions. She now produced a small loaf of bread and cut it into four pieces. I was hungry, but I simply could not eat it—my throat was stone-dry, and at that moment I would have done anything for a tall glass of cool, refreshing water. That night, my little siblings cried constantly. They, too, were thirstier than they had ever been.

My mother turned her head so we wouldn't see her tears. How could a mother bear to hear her own children scream for water? Her heart was being ripped to pieces. Other families were in the same predicament, and I heard cries from everywhere. Thirst, too, was a weapon of annihilation in the arsenal of the Turkish government, which was silently enacting its genocidal plan before the indifference of the world.

The poor deportees who had survived their journey to Hama now melted into the desert sand. Some did manage to escape to the nearby village of Salamieh,* and others headed toward Homs or Damascus, or even to Tripoli and to Beirut, where many had relatives. If they didn't survive, they at least found a more honorable end. Those who were fated to remain in the camp paid the ultimate price.

As the epidemics continued, the number of mothers dwindled, while the number of orphans surged. Hundreds of children wandered around the camp, having lost everyone, dying slowly and without a whimper, their eyes accusing all mankind.

The most naive among us believed the rumors about the imminent conclusion of the war, and even made preparations to go back home. But we had already packed our bags so many times, and there seemed no end to our open-air imprisonment.

At night, we could lie down in the sand and get a few hours of sleep. In our dreams, we all flew back home. Alas, we always eventually woke to the nightmare that was our lives.

૭

At dawn, my sister was shrieking. It sounded like someone was suffocating her. I jumped up. Was a stranger trying to kidnap her? No, it was my own mother, whose stiff arms were grasping my sister's neck. My grandmother was struggling to free my sister, and my grandfather ran in to help. They saved my sister, who was screaming at the top of her lungs. As she calmed down, we realized that my mother was not moving—it looked like she was sleeping peacefully, something she probably had not experienced for weeks.

---

* Salamieh is al-Salamiyya, southeast of Hama and northeast of Homs.

My grandmother immediately took us away, putting us into the care of Garbo Emmi's family.

The women of my family gathered around my mother's lifeless body, beating their chests and tearing out their hair. They covered my mother with a white sheet and continued crying and praying over her for the entire day. At some point, I couldn't take it anymore, and the emotions that had been building up within me for months finally erupted. I began crying, and I couldn't stop. My brother and sister soon joined me, and we wailed for many hours.

That day we received no bread. The family had none. Garbo Emmi's daughters spent the entire day with us. They were clearly suffering, too, and seemed on the edge of breaking down, but they did their best to seem calm before us.

As night fell, my grandmother came to fetch us back. Where my mother's bed had been, there was nothing but sand and dirt. My little brother, only three years old, kept staring at the empty space. In a daze, I traced my mother's figure in the sand—the outline of her head, her torso, her arms, her legs. When I finished, I looked at my handiwork, which only confirmed that she was gone forever.

I could still see her sitting there, my little siblings on her knees, smiling, praying, and dividing the bread among us all. In her eyes, in her smiles, was all the love and goodness of the world.

My grandmother became our primary caretaker. Now that we were orphaned, she redoubled her efforts to care for our every need. She buried her own pain, and she made us her only priority. All day, all she thought about was how to procure food and water for us, how to make our lives slightly more comfortable in the desert hell. My grandfather, too, lived through us. After touring the camp to encourage his people, he always returned to us, stroked our hair, asked us how we were doing, and blessed us.

Krikor, in addition to serving as the literal breadwinner of the family, played with us whenever he had free time. Collectively, they did their best to replace my mother, to emulate the love she had given us. They meant well, but at night, my poor mother would appear before me in my dreams; she would smile at me, then fade away into the darkness when I ran toward her.

Less than a week later, my sister burned up with fever. She stayed in bed all day, groaning and tossing. Her skin turned red, and she constantly opened and closed her mouth like a suffocating fish. She babbled, speaking to no one in particular, and seemed to hallucinate. She repeated our names. Perhaps she wanted to ask us something. Once in a while she opened her eyes and looked all around her.

"She's looking for her mother," whispered my grandmother. She took my sister into her lap to try to rock her to sleep.

My grandfather, my uncle, and my aunt could offer no words of comfort or the usual assurances that she would be fine. They stood there in despair. There were neither doctors nor medication in the camp. What could we do to help the unfortunate girl?

"Her eyes are glazing over. She won't last long," murmured my aunt, and in fact my sister did not bear her cross much longer. She closed her eyes one last time, and she was gone. An hour or two later, the cart that collected corpses rolled by, and we tossed her body onto it. It was done. The cart rolled away. My brother and I had no more tears to cry. Within four days, I had lost my mother and my sister. My father had vanished long ago. The only remains of our once happy family were my brother and me.

We felt hollow and numb. My grandmother, under the weight of the stress and misery, fell ill. Now she was the one who needed care, and we were terrified that she, too, would follow her daughter and granddaughter into the afterworld.

Sahag and Garo had died, too, within two days of each other. I had lost everything. My mind was a beehive of horrified thoughts, all jostling with each other and consuming my brain. Where could I go? Whom could I turn to for help? I was only five years old, but I had seen more suffering and death than most people witness during their entire lives.

Then strange spots appeared on my brother's forehead and cheeks. At first the spots were small, but they developed into large, ominous red circles and spread all over his body. He had a fever, and he became extremely lethargic. He constantly asked for water. We watched him toss and turn, lying on a small rug, scratching himself and screaming from thirst. Thankfully, he didn't suffer for long. Within hours, a final convulsion rocked his body. He exhaled his last breath.

"Brother! Little brother!" I yelled to his lifeless form, losing my head completely. Once again, my grandmother took me away to stay with my uncle's family. A little later, from a distance, I saw the familiar cart, with my brother's body lying on top. My last remaining link to my past life, my last vestige of innocence and happiness, was gone.

I sat beside my grandmother, the weight of the world on my shoulders. I felt forsaken in the world, with no idea what fate awaited me. I sat still all day. I didn't respond to my grandmother's questions. I was barely aware of what was happening around me. At night, I lay down, tormented by my thoughts until I drifted off into a death-like stupor.

I spent the following days in a daze. My loneliness was suffocating me. At nights, I woke up screaming and unable to return to sleep. I sometimes hallucinated that I was in the presence of my mother and siblings.

The death cart could no longer keep pace with the corpses. Stacked with dead bodies, it headed toward the ditches and hillocks in the desert. There, the bodies were just thrown into small caves or buried in shallow graves.

The cart-pusher could no longer bear it. One day, I heard him complain to some of the elders: "I can't do it any longer! As God is my witness, I can't go on!" he cried. "I swear, I would rather burn in the fires of hell than continue doing this. Why can't someone else do it?" The man couldn't be blamed. For weeks, he had been doing the job out of the goodness of his heart, never receiving a penny for his pains.

One morning, Krikor went to fetch bread again. We had eaten our last crumbs the night before, and we were all very hungry. When he returned, he was covered in bruises again.

"What happened, my son?" asked his mother.

"The guards beat us," whimpered Krikor, wiping the tears from his eyes.

"Why did they do that?"

"They said we shouldn't go there for bread anymore."

"But why?" asked my grandmother.

"They said people won't bring bread anymore. They've forbidden it."

The news spread like wildfire, naturally resulting in great consternation among the exiles.

"They're trying to starve us to death!" yelled one woman.

"It must be an order from the government!" added another.

"But this is sheer murder!" said Vartan Emmi.

"What are we going to do? Who'll help us now?" asked someone.

"The devil! God has forsaken us. The devil's the only one we can pray to now," answered Kevork Emmi. Nobody had the energy to admonish him for his blasphemous words, which, in a time of peace, would have scandalized anyone who heard them.

"This is a trick of the guards! They're trying to extort money from us. They're Turks, after all," muttered Toros Emmi, gritting his teeth.

My grandfather took a few elders with him to speak to the guards, figuring that he could bribe them, if necessary. They were slow to return, and we grew even more anxious. Finally, the old men appeared over a dune. As soon as they reached us and sat down, dozens of the women surrounded them.

My grandfather spoke with a sardonic smile.

"They treated us with utter disrespect. They told us the bread would come and made us wait for hours. Then when it became clear that it was an empty promise, they said it had been a mistake, and that we would get bread tomorrow."

"One of the soldiers was sitting under a tree, smoking an elegant water pipe," added Garbo Emmi. "We asked him why we had not gotten bread today. He sneered and cursed, 'You should be satisfied that we even let you live. You want bread? Why don't you pray to your God? There's no bread in the city, the bakeries are all closed, and the Turks are hungry, yet we're supposed to give *you* bread? We should strike you down for such insolence!'"

Many went pale and shed silent tears. "What have we done to deserve this?" lamented Vartan Emmi.

The women exchanged terrified glances. At that moment, a breeze blew, bringing with it the stench of the dead, as if reminding us that we, too, would soon be buried in the desert sand.

The orphans lined up in the courtyard of the Antoura orphanage, ca. 1916.

Source: Photo courtesy of Missak Kelechian, Collège Saint Joseph—Antoura.

The Antoura College, Lebanon, was established by Jesuit priests in 1656 and later taken over by the Lazarist order. It was converted from 1915 to 1918 into an orphanage for Armenian and Kurdish youth by the Ottoman government.

Source: Photo courtesy of Missak Kelechian, Collège Saint Joseph–Antoura.

Jemal Pasha (*center front*), commander of the Turkish Fourth Army in Syria, and Halide Edip (*right front*) stand with other dignitaries at the steps of the French College at Antoura, Lebanon, 1916.

Source: Photo from the collection Dr. Bayard Dodge. Courtesy of Missak Kelechian, Collège Saint Joseph–Antoura.

The orphans playing in the courtyard of the Antoura orphanage, likely after the departure of the Turkish administrators and the arrival of the American Near East Relief workers, ca. 1919.

Source: Photo courtesy of Missak Kelechian, Collège Saint Joseph–Antoura.

Ray Travis (*upper left, the only man wearing a Western-style hat*), with the Armenian orphans at the Millet Khan Orphanage in Aintab, 1919. Travis (1906–1965), a missionary and civil servant, served in World War I in France, and then undertook relief work as a missionary in Aintab. He later became director of the Near East Relief Orphanage in Jbeil, Lebanon.

Source: Photo courtesy of Garo Derounian, Armenian Genocide and Orphans Museum at Birds Nest, Jbeil, Lebanon. Reprinted by permission.

Karnig Panian (*seated, fourth from right*) with some of the former orphans of the Orphanage of Jbeil, Lebanon, 1968. The Orphanage of Jbeil was governed by the American Near East Relief from 1920 to 1925.

CHAPTER 4

THE ORPHANAGE AT HAMA

ONE MORNING, I noticed my grandfather and Garbo Emmi in a corner, whispering to each other, looking very concerned and anxious. Soon they called over my grandmother, who joined their discussion.

"No! I won't hear of it! I don't want him taken away!" she cried. "I know we're going hungry, I know we have no water, but it's better to die together! Better that than separation!"

But after some time, my grandfather and Garbo Emmi convinced my grandmother.

Garbo Emmi walked over to me, grasped my hand, and prepared to lead me away. I didn't know where we were going. My grandmother threw her arms around me and began to cry. My grandfather silently stroked my hair, then kissed me again and again. Finally, all four of us walked to the perimeter of the camp.

"Halt! Where are you going? Where are you taking the boy?" asked a guard.

"We're taking him to the orphanage in town," replied Garbo Emmi.

"Fine. But you come back right away," assented the guard.

"I give you my word of honor," answered Garbo Emmi, and we walked out of the camp, leaving my grandparents behind. Within minutes, we reached a one-story house. Garbo Emmi knocked on the door. From within I heard the shrieks and laughter of other boys.

A modestly dressed man stood in the doorway. After exchanging a few words with Garbo Emmi, he took me by the hand and led me inside. When I turned back after a few moments, the door was closed and Garbo Emmi was gone.

The man took me into his office and explained where I was. The other boys staying in the house were just like me—they had also lost their parents. This institution was an orphanage, and he was the headmaster. Soon he handed me over to a few women, who took away my dirty rags and clothed me in clean underwear, pants, shirt, and coat. They didn't bathe me, because they had no water. When I was ready, the headmaster took me out to the courtyard. I saw fifty or sixty boys, all approximately my age. They all wore the same type of coat, which was used as a uniform, and their heads had been shaved. I remembered some of them, as well as some of the women who worked there, from the camp.

The building itself consisted of five or six large rooms, which doubled as dormitories and storerooms, as well as a larger room used as a kitchen and mess hall. We played outside, in the courtyard, which was fenced in by a high wall.

The headmaster was a Protestant pastor. He constantly patrolled the courtyard, keeping an eye on us. I marveled at his kindness. He never had to reprimand any of the boys; they all respected him so much that his mere presence was enough to ensure order.

This man spent almost his every waking hour with us: he supervised the preparation of the meals and the washing of the bedsheets, regaled us with stories and folktales, kept an eye on our health, and even inspected our scalps, looking for lice.

He was a sanguine, happy man. No matter what tragedies he encountered, he put his faith in God and never succumbed to despair—after all, everything was part of the Lord's plan. He constantly read the Bible and often gave us sermons inspired by the Holy Book. There was no doubt that he loved children. Wasn't his orphanage the noblest expression of that love?

My first day there, at noon, we all gathered in the mess hall for lunch. Each boy was given a large piece of fresh bread and a bowl of gruel. It was delicious—absolutely delicious! I had not had soup for months. The women lunched with us, too.

After lunch, I had my first interactions with my new peers. They were from all different parts of the country, and some spoke dialects that I could barely understand. I met three boys named Hovhannes, Sahag, and Kalust, all from Sepastia. They were all slightly older than me, but they proved to be trustworthy friends. That first evening, several more new boys were brought to the orphanage, and the schoolmaster kindly welcomed them.

The next morning, right after breakfast, a barber headed straight for me. My hair had grown very long, and he sheared it all off, leaving me practically bald, like all the other boys.

There were knocks at the door—more new orphans came in. Within a few days, our number reached a hundred. We still had enough food for everyone, and we slept three to a bed. Given the circumstances, we felt like we were living in the lap of luxury.

At noon, the headmaster appeared at the doorway, a bell in his hand. When he rang the bell, all the boys lined up before him. At a gesture by the pastor, we moved forward into another room, and we each took a seat at a chair with a bowl before it. One of the older boys stood and recited the Hayr Mer. At the end of the prayer, he made the sign of the cross, a movement mimicked by the others. We began eating. We had another delicious hot meal: potato soup. We were even allowed seconds. I almost felt embarrassed—it had been so long since I had eaten to my heart's content.

"Keep eating! They'll take the food away soon!" said the boy to my left as he shoveled soup into his mouth.

I couldn't eat any more, so I left my bowl unfinished and ran out to the courtyard to play. The others had already separated into different groups and were playing all kinds of games. Our joyful voices proved that we still had the ability to enjoy life. We had almost forgotten that we were exiles and that the remnants of our families were still stuck in that terrible camp. We were children again.

But at night, I often dreamed of my family. I felt an acute sense of guilt: I was enjoying a clean bed and full stomach, while they were still suffering, still hungry and sleepless, still tormented by thirst and the desert heat. Were they getting any bread and water? Had Krikor recovered from his latest violent encounter with the guards? Who was dead, and who was still alive? Had the bodies of my mother, brother, and sister been lost under thousands of new corpses in those horrid, fetid ditches?

⌣

One day, while we were in the courtyard, we heard wild screams from the outside. The terrible, chaotic din grew louder with every minute, coming closer and closer. For the traumatized boys, it was a reminder of what they had escaped. We froze in our tracks, listening in terror, conjuring hellish scenes in our imagination. Many of us had heard similar sounds on our way to the deportee camp, when caravans had been attacked by sword-wielding crowds of bloodthirsty Turks. What was happening out there? Were they killing again? Robbing?

As the cacophony approached, panic overtook some of the boys. It sounded like a mob was coming straight for us. We heard sounds of running feet, objects striking the outside wall, and people pushing and shoving. We heard women and children begging for their lives, and we heard some of them silenced in mid-sentence.

At any moment, this mob might break down the gates and pour in. What would happen to us?

The pastor appeared among us, his expression betraying his own terror. The orphans surrounded him, hoping that his presence would somehow protect them. We clung to his arms and legs. By now, all of us were in tears. We were lost, or so we thought.

Fortunately, over the next few minutes, the noise faded away, and the mob moved on. Nobody broke in. The pastor took a deep breath of relief and tried to reassure us that we were safe.

Later that day, he received visitors who explained that starving people had gotten wind of a shipment of bread that had arrived in town, destined for the army at the front. The civilian population attacked the soldiers guarding the shipment and tried to steal the bread. The mob pleaded with the soldiers, begging for pity. The guards aimed their guns at the crowd, and according to some they fired, which ignited complete chaos in the streets. Most of the victims were local Arabs.

The Armenian deportees weren't the only ones who were dying of hunger. Famine gripped the entire city of Hama—which implied, of course, that no bread had been sold to those in the camp, including the few remaining members of my own family.

Soon, hunger infiltrated the orphanage, too. In the beginning, we had received three meals per day. Then we started getting two meals a day—a light breakfast of bread and tea, and supper at four in the afternoon, consisting of bread and a few pieces of potato with chunks of meat, or rice and meat. Fruit disappeared from our diet. Still, we were content with what we received, as we had experienced much worse in the camp.

At this point, the orphanage was still accepting two or three new orphans per day. The pastor didn't have the heart to turn anybody away. Our number rose beyond a hundred and fifty and approached two hundred.

In the shops and the market, food became more and more scarce. Fruit and cereals were rare and, when found, exorbitantly expensive. Our caretakers were sent out on a daily basis, and they usually returned empty-handed. Even the children realized that famine was a real threat. Two hundred of them had to be fed every day, and there was fear that the number of daily meals would be decreased to one.

One morning we woke up and found that the pastor had left the orphanage without saying a word. The period of his absence was a nightmare for the boys. We asked the caretakers where he was, but they didn't know.

A day passed, then two, then three; still, the pastor did not reappear. Thankfully there was enough to eat in the storerooms of the orphanage, and some kind people from the city brought us bread. We had bread and tea in the morning, and in the afternoon we ate beans, potatoes, or lentils without meat. We didn't protest. All of the boys were on their best behavior, while the women all continued to treat us as their own children.

On the fourth day, the pastor finally appeared. When he walked into the orphanage, looking the worse for wear, we quickly surrounded him. We were his sons, and our father had returned from a long absence. He greeted us with warm embraces and reassuring words.

With him he brought two carts full of food, which were waiting outside the gate. The older boys helped carry the supplies into the courtyard and to the supply rooms. The pastor now explained that he had ventured to the nearby village of Salamieh and succeeded in buying large amounts of food.

That evening, during dinner, the pastor expressed his great pleasure at hearing that we had behaved well during his absence. He then told a few jokes to lift our spirits.

The orphanage was once again in peace. However, new orphans were still brought in, and they told terrible stories of what was occurring inside the camp. We gradually became persuaded that none of our remaining relatives would survive.

Then, one morning, to my great surprise and relief, my grandparents came to visit. They saw that I was doing well, that I had even gained some weight. They said that everyone was still alive, including Krikor and Ardashes.

"Is Krikor able to get bread? Are they selling any at the camp?" I asked.

"He goes every day, waits for hours, then gets as much as he can. We all split up what he buys," replied my grandfather.

"They give us food twice a day here!" I proudly stated.

"That's marvelous, my dear," smiled my grandmother.

"Our pastor went and got some food from the villages just the other day," I continued to brag.

"May God grant that pastor a long life," blessed my grandmother.

They had a strange, wistful expression in their eyes. I think they were thankful that at least I would survive the deportations, and they believed that the rest of the family was already condemned.

As they were leaving, my grandfather produced a handful of *leblebi*[*] from his pocket and slipped it into mine. Then, they kissed me and left. My

---

[*] A snack of roasted chickpeas.

grandfather remained stoic, but at the last moment, my grandmother broke into tears.

Knowing that they were going back to hunger and misery, how could I eat the leblebi by myself? I handed each of my friends a few, then ate the rest sadly, before we all returned to our games.

◡

After the riot, we lived in peace, though we never left the orphanage. A few days later, a small squadron of troops appeared at the gate, accompanied by two officers on horseback. These two sauntered into the courtyard while their men waited outside.

It was breakfast time, and one of the boys was reciting the Hayr Mer when the two officers barged into the room. The pastor jumped to his feet, saluted the soldiers, and led them to his office.

We couldn't hide our fear. All the orphans had unpleasant experiences with uniformed Turkish officers. The orphanage walls had sheltered us from them. They were now invading our last safe space.

The conversation between the pastor and the officers went on for a while. Outside, in the courtyard, we couldn't play. We waited anxiously. Doubt and terror crept into our minds. The mere presence of the Turkish troops had jarred us.

Finally, the door of the pastor's office creaked open. The orphans gathered in the corners of the courtyard, terrified. The officers walked out of the gate, jumped onto their horses, and trotted away with their infantry escort. The pastor walked over to us, an immeasurable sadness in his eyes. We had never seen him so dismayed. He seemed on the verge of breaking into tears.

"Play on, boys," he said, then walked back into his office and closed the door behind him.

Obviously, something had completely upended him. Usually, during recess time, he patrolled the courtyard, watching our games, flashing his encouraging smile. It was very unusual for him to stay in his office for hours. We didn't even see him before we retired to bed. He had the habit of gathering us together before we went to bed, telling us parables and allegories from the Bible. But on that night, he failed to appear in our bedrooms.

Our female caretakers, too, were experts at cheering us up. They spent hours telling us folktales in which the good characters always won, while the evil ones always got their just punishment. Sometimes, we wondered why in *our* story, the good were still suffering while the perpetrators of evil were prospering.

"Don't worry, boys, their turn will come, too, and God will punish them," these good women told us. "God will always be the final judge."

"Will that happen soon, Mayrig?" we asked.

"Don't ever lose your hope, boys," they said.

೫

About a week later, the Turkish officers returned and had another short conversation with the pastor. When they left, he looked like a defeated, hopeless man. He spoke with three of the older boys. When these three came out to the courtyard, we surrounded them and bombarded them with questions. "The pastor didn't tell us anything," said one of them, and they walked away, clearly troubled.

We chatted in whispers, wondering what new hell awaited us, and we cast occasional worried glances toward the gate, through which the Turkish officers were sure to return. We were well aware that our fates completely depended on those officers.

Eventually, as the days rolled by, the three boys could no longer protect us from the bad news. They began dropping hints, until we knew quite well what was going to happen. Jemal Pasha, the military commander in the area, was taking the Armenian orphans to Lebanon. According to the officers, the pasha was a kind, compassionate man who wanted to educate the boys and make men of them. Out of the apparent kindness of his heart, he had even appropriated some of the army's own food supply for use in this new orphanage dedicated to educating Armenian boys.

Within three or four days, we would be forced to leave the haven of the orphanage. We would leave our relatives and families, at least those still alive in the camp, and be taken away from our new father, the pastor, who had provided us with comfort and safety. We were petrified. The pastor had made it clear to the three boys that he doubted Jemal Pasha's credentials as a "kind, compassionate" man—and if the pastor doubted, how could we believe?

The younger orphans barely understood what was going on around them, but they did realize that once again they would be taken away, losing another home and hearth. The older boys pondered the feasibility of returning to the camp. "Better to die than to become Turks," they figured. "We should go back to the camp to die with our grandparents and our mothers." When the pastor opened the gate to accept more new orphans, two of the older boys slipped out and ran for the camp. No one chased them down.

This first successful attempt emboldened others. Two days later, some boys were preparing to make their own escape, but the pastor got wind of their plan. "What are you thinking, boys?" he chided. "Do you really believe you'd be better off in that camp? What about the others you're leaving behind? What about the little ones? Wherever you go, don't you think they'll need your help? Who else is going to watch over them?"

The pastor's words struck a chord.

"We won't run away! We'll stay here with everyone!" said one boy, his voice shaking with emotion. "We won't ever abandon the younger boys. We promise."

༄

One evening, before supper, as we played in the courtyard, the pastor came outside and stood in one corner, watching us with great sadness in his eyes. It looked like he wanted to say something to us. Eventually, he signaled to some of the older boys to gather around him. He asked them to come to his office, where he sat down, and the boys sat around him. At first, he couldn't speak. Tears welled in his eyes, and his lips trembled. Eventually, he forced himself to regain his composure and spoke: "My boys. My dear boys. Tonight, we will eat together for the last time under this roof. Early tomorrow morning, we'll head to the train station, and you'll be taken to a country called Lebanon.

You will be the first orphans accepted into Jemal Pasha's new orphanage." He had to pause, then continued, "I have been assured that Jemal Pasha will take good care of you, educate you, and make sure you grow up to be good men."

"Up until now, you have been my own sons," he said. His eyes were closed, as if in silent meditation. "You are Armenian children, and you will always be Armenian. Whatever happens, do not ever forget your language and your prayers. Do not ever lose your faith. God has protected you, and I am sure he will be watching over you in the future, wherever you are taken. Do not weaken, do not yield, and do not lose hope. Whenever in doubt, rely on each other's support, and rely on God, who, I assure you, will always hear your prayers."

The boys were in tears. The pastor bade us all to go to bed. We stayed up late into the night, sitting on our beds and chatting gloomily. Some were already speculating on the next gauntlet that we were to pass through.

It was past midnight when we went to sleep. Early the next morning, the pastor's voice roused us from our beds. We gathered in the courtyard. We had no baggage to take with us, just the clothes on our backs. A dozen Turkish troops waited for us outside the gates. Their sight sent shivers down our spines. The troops were to escort us to the train. Two of them led the column while the others surrounded us, presumably to prevent any of us from making a run for it. The train station was only a few hundred feet away.

To our left was the dark silhouette of the camp, and beyond it the desert, with its caves full of Armenian corpses. The toxic stench of rotting flesh was in the air.

⁓

A large crowd gathered at the train station. The relatives of the orphans had learned of the planned deportation, and they came to bid farewell to their sons and grandsons. I saw my grandfather and my grandmother, as well as my aunt and my cousins. They were not allowed to approach us. There were many tears on both sides, but no physical contact was allowed.

We were lined up right outside the main entrance of the station. Suddenly, there was disorder inside. Officials and soldiers were lining up, too, in two rows. As a group of officers passed between these two rows, the soldiers clicked their heels and saluted. One of the officers was a tall, large man, his chest bedecked with medals and decorations, a sword dangling from his hip. He was followed by several adjutants.

This officer smiled at us and then exchanged a few words with our pastor. The orphans didn't dare move a muscle. It seemed like our fate was being decided then and there by this strange, obviously important man.

When he walked back to the reception area of the station, the crowds followed, and there was almost a stampede. In the chaos, my grandfather, grandmother, and aunt were able to get to me. They kissed me, embraced me, and cried. My grandfather furtively pushed Krikor into our ranks and said, "Krikor will come with you to keep a watch over you."

I was elated. I would not be alone. I had a trusted cousin beside me.

The train whistled. The soldiers pushed the crowd back and cleared a path for us. The second whistle came, and a soldier ordered us to get on board. The pastor and our caretakers kissed us all and bade us farewell, and there were many emotional outbursts on both sides. We boarded the train, and with the third whistle, we began moving.

As the train chugged forward at breakneck speed, we found ourselves crossing a vast desert. There was nobody to be seen, no homes or towns on either side of the tracks.

Aboard that train were the last remaining sons of an annihilated nation, racing toward unknown shores, tossed about by the waves of fate. All that was left of our families and hometowns were our memories.

At our first stop, in the town of Homs, some other passengers alighted, and new ones boarded the train with their luggage. Most were poor country folk in tattered clothing and shoes. A ripe odor of sweat filled the wagons, rendering it almost intolerable. After a while the soldier in our wagon couldn't take it anymore, and he pulled the door slightly ajar to let in some fresh air.

We were soon winding our way upward into the mountains. The train groaned as it climbed, leaving behind a thick wake of smoke. The whistle echoed in the darkening mountains. At least we were leaving behind that hellish desert and that terrible stench of death.

At the stop in Baalbek,* some locals sold bread and fruit. When they saw that the wagons were full of famished children, these kind people threw baskets of bread and fruit into the wagons without asking for any payment. The older boys judiciously divided everything among the orphans. We hadn't eaten all day. Now we had not only bread but also fresh apricots, grapes, and prunes.

"Who knows when we'll eat again? Stuff yourselves, boys!" exclaimed one boy as he crammed his mouth with bread.

The train whistled again and chugged on. We crossed orchards and fields, and then more mountains again. We climbed slowly, and the descent was even slower. The sun was already setting. It was dark when the train, whistling several times, screeched to a halt in Beirut.

We were given bread and told to board another train, which waited on a parallel set of tracks. With Krikor by my side, holding my hand, the second train whistled and began moving. It seemed that we were traveling in the opposite direction. Soon we were racing alongside the sea. In the darkness of the waves on our left, we could see lights bobbing up and down. The soldier in the wagon said these were fishermen.

On our right, we saw some lights out of the train's windows, which relieved us. It meant we were not going back into a desert. People lived here, at least. The train slowed down and eventually came to a halt. We had reached our terminus, but apparently, our final destination was still quite a distance away.

Directed by the soldiers, we started walking. There were blind boys among us, so some of the older boys took their arms and guided them forward. The youngest boys, too, held the older ones' hands to keep pace and avoid getting lost in the darkness. The road was narrow, and it climbed into hills. We often slid on the gravel. At last, we stopped in the square of a small village. We thought we had arrived, but we were wrong.

"We still have half an hour to go!" called the soldier in the lead.

We kept going, barely able to drag ourselves forward. Half an hour

---

* Baalbek is a major town in the Beqaa Valley of Lebanon.

passed, but we were not there yet. We passed through orchards and farmland. Finally, we reached a small village, with a dozen or so shops in its center.

"We're here!" called out the soldier in the lead, stopping in front of a large, new building. We breathed a sigh. Some of the orphans had walked barefoot, and the stones and gravel had bloodied their feet, but now the suffering was over.

At the entrance of the building, a few women greeted us in Turkish and invited us inside. We followed the women up the stairs. In the darkness, we couldn't see much, but we realized that this building would be our home for the foreseeable future. This was the orphanage in Antoura.

We entered a gigantic dormitory occupied by long rows of beds. We hadn't slept in such comfortable beds since leaving our homes. They had thick blankets and clean sheets. Even at the orphanage in Hama, our beds had been relatively primitive and uncomfortable.

Maybe Jemal Pasha was determined to care for us properly, after all. But we didn't give it much thought, since we were so exhausted. Krikor and I crawled into a bed together, and we quickly dozed off.

CHAPTER 5

THE ORPHANAGE AT ANTOURA

THE SUN HAD ALREADY RISEN when we woke up. Out the door and across the hallway I could see another large room lined with beds. There were more such rooms down the hallway. Together they contained hundreds of beds. We washed in a lavatory and then went downstairs and out into the courtyard. In its center was a clock tower. In one corner was a small chapel. There were various statues of saints. Clearly, we were in a religious institution or monastery that had been transformed into an orphanage.[*]

There was a separate, two-story building right across from the chapel, presumably reserved for staff members and teachers. On the first floor of the main building were about forty small rooms. These would be our classrooms.

The courtyard was our playground. Squeezed between the main building and the staff building, it was small, but it was good enough for us. There was also a small building used as a gymnasium, and in one corner of the courtyard was a sundial.

The orphanage was located on the peak of a hill, overlooking orchards and fields. I looked down toward them, jealously glaring at the heavy, ripe fruit and the terraces of vegetables.

The sun was already high in the sky when a few women approached us

---

[*] The institution was Collège Saint Joseph, established in 1834 by French Lazarist priests.

with smiles. They began speaking to some of the older boys in Turkish. They apparently said that we would always have to speak Turkish in this orphanage, and that their job was to teach us the language.

I was troubled. I didn't know a word of Turkish. Back home, we had always spoken Armenian; even the local Turks had learned it. Here, everything was upside down. I looked around fearfully, like a lost sheep.

At the sound of a bell, we were made to stand in line. I was placed among other boys my age, and one of the women motioned to us to enter the main building. We went down the steps and found ourselves in a large mess hall.

There were two very long tables, stretching all the way across the hall, and benches on either side of them. We sat down, all two hundred of us, and a bowl was placed before each orphan.

A few minutes later some older women appeared carrying buns of bread in baskets. They gave us each one bun, and then another woman placed six or seven olives in each bowl. The pieces of bread we received were smaller than the ones we had received at the Hama orphanage, but we didn't complain. We didn't say grace; we were told to begin eating. This was apparently the custom here. The bread and the olives were devoured within a few minutes.

Outside in the courtyard, we spoke Armenian whenever the Turkish women weren't around. But we did so with fear. We knew we were breaking the rules.

At first, whenever these women caught us, they would kindly but insistently exhort us: *Türkçe konuşun güzelim!* "Speak Turkish, my dear!" I didn't quite know what these words meant, but they were repeated so many times that I memorized them.

Soon the women became much more insistent, urging *Türkçe konuşun* whenever they saw us whispering. But we kept speaking Armenian—it was the only language we knew.

Less than two weeks after our arrival, another group of orphans arrived at the institution. They were all Armenian, and among them were some girls our age. Then a third group arrived, boys and girls, most of them older than me, between the age of eight and ten. The girls were not kept with us.

Their dormitories were in separate buildings. We seldom saw them. Were they from Hama? All we knew was that they, too, had lost their parents.

Within a month of our arrival, more than five hundred orphans were at Antoura. During that month, much had changed. In the first place, the administration had decided to get rid of our names and replace them with Turkish ones.

One morning, after breakfast, we lined up and were taken into the headmaster's office in groups of five. The headmaster, Fevzi Bey,* was seated behind a large bureau cluttered with books and stationery. We stood before him, staring at the floor like guilty criminals waiting to hear their verdicts. He began speaking grandiloquently, though I could only understand a few of his words. The gist of his speech was that we would now have to forget our old names and receive new ones. This change signified the beginning of our transformation into proud Turks. Alongside our new names, we would also each receive a number.

I didn't know Turkish, nor did I know any Turkish names, or even the Turkish names of numbers. All I knew was my true name, and I didn't see the point of changing it. The boy before me was asked his name, and he replied with his Armenian name. Without warning, Fevzi Bey smacked him right across the face. The boy fell to the ground and began crying. His nose was bleeding.

Furious, the headmaster screamed at him: "Forget your old name! Forget it! From now on, your name will be Ahmet, and your number will be 549!" The other boys in the room were shaking like leaves. It was my turn next. I said my name was Karnig. Now it was my turn to be slapped across the face and fall to the floor, crying. The schoolmaster then kicked my sides as I lay prostrate on the floor. I eventually passed out from the pain.

When I came to, I was lying in a bed. I had never been in this room. I saw more orphans, each lying in a bed of his own. I couldn't see very well, and I shut my eyes again and fell back asleep. Two days later, I found out that I was in the clinic, and that I had been the first orphan brought there.

---

* *Bey* is a courtesy title, formerly applied to the governor of a district or province in the Ottoman Empire.

Krikor came to visit me. He sat at the edge of the bed and slipped a piece of bread under my pillow. He told me that he had found a job in the storeroom. "From now on, we'll never be hungry. I'll bring you bread every day," he promised.

I don't know how many days I spent in that bed. My ribs throbbed with pain. There were no doctors and no medication. Every few days, a kindly old lady would come by, stroke my hair, say some things in Turkish, then move on to the next patient.

At noon, they gave us each a piece of bread and a cup of water. I barely ate—even the bread Krikor brought me remained under my pillow. I had no appetite. When a few days later I tried to eat the bread they had given me, I could barely chew it; it was terribly hard, and it didn't taste like anything I had eaten before. I chewed the hard mass as best as I could, then went back to sleep. I didn't want to be awake.

One day, the woman making the rounds in the clinic made me move my arms and my legs. Discovering that I was no longer in pain, she proclaimed that I could be dismissed from the clinic.

I walked out of the infirmary and went out into the courtyard. A teacher saw me loitering in the hallway. She grabbed me and took me inside her classroom. The boys in the class were packed onto benches like sardines. Most of them were older than me, and they were making quite a racket. The teacher tried to impose silence—she kept yelling and striking her table with her large wooden ruler.

The other classrooms sounded just as chaotic. We could hear cries, beatings, and threats from the teachers. "If you don't calm down, I'll gouge your eyes out!" screamed our teacher, standing before a particularly unruly boy. "You aren't students, you're all dolts!" she squealed before striking the boy on the head with her wooden ruler.

"What am I going to do in a classroom like this?" I thought to myself. "I don't know Turkish. I don't even have the slightest clue how to speak it! Our school in our town had been such a marvelous place, but here, these teachers seem more interested in becoming our torturers than our educators."

The bell rang, indicating the end of the lesson. It was already noon and it was hot outside. The orphans ran out of the classroom, down into the court-yard, and congregated in the shade of the trees. There was much to talk about.

"They'll see," one of the boys threatened. "If they try to hit me again tomorrow, I'll rip my uniform up and . . ."

"Are we hostages?" asked another. "Are we slaves? They're torturing us!"

"You better not be late tomorrow, or they'll turn you into a bloody pulp," another boy warned me. He took my hand and showed me the location of my new classroom.

We received lunch at eleven in the morning, then dinner at five o'clock. Usually we got a small piece of dark bread and a bowl of what looked like soup, although we could never figure out what it contained other than boiled water. We certainly couldn't judge based on flavor—it was totally bland. Regardless, we ate as much as possible. At first, when there were about two hundred orphans, they gave us enough to fill our stomachs, but as the number of orphans rose, past four hundred and then six hundred, both the quantity and the quality of the food took a turn for worse.

The next morning, when the bell rang, I went into the correct class-room. When the teacher walked in, she had a kind smile on her face. Her eyes were large and expressive, and she wore her hair in a ponytail. At first sight, she was the exact opposite of the violent teacher I had witnessed the day before. Then my eyes moved to the long ruler in her hand. How could such a motherly, gentle creature hold such a sadistic weapon of pain?

The teacher began lecturing. I couldn't understand a word, though I sat still, afraid of what would happen if I showed any sign of inattention. My peers, too, seem to be listening intently to her. Unfortunately, the other classes must not have been behaving so well. Again and again, we heard the cries of *Eşek! Köpek!* "Donkey! Dog!"

Later, outside, the older boys regaled us with stories of their classroom exploits. They had angered their teachers and been harshly punished; in fact, many had been severely beaten, but they didn't care. Even at this point, some of the braver ones brazenly spoke Armenian and addressed each other with their Armenian names.

"They want to make Turks out of us! But it'll never work with me! My name isn't Mehmet! We won't turn into Turks!" cried out one of the more excitable orphans.

"We won't! We won't!" came the vociferous reply from others.

It was an unequal battle between the administration and the students. Clearly, Jemal Pasha's plan was to Turkify us, but we were determined to resist—not out of rabid nationalism, for which we were too young, but simply because we wanted to hold onto our identities, which were all we had left.

༄

When we entered the mess hall, the clever and quick boys always rushed to the front of the long table, where they received their bread first, which meant it was always warmer and fresher. Once we were sitting, there was no way to keep order in the mess hall. It was utter chaos.

One day, we were particularly excited because we heard that we would be served meat and potatoes. In the excitement, an Armenian word slipped out of my mouth. For weeks I had remained mute, terrified of punishment and beatings, and now I had committed the cardinal sin at the Antoura Orphanage.

The boy sitting beside me nudged me in the ribs, and I immediately realized what I had done. Thankfully, none of the staff had heard me. Otherwise I probably wouldn't get any meat and potatoes!

It was finally our table's turn to be served. We received the usual meager bun of bread. Then, to our delight, we each got a ladleful of stew. Excitedly, I grabbed my spoon and inspected the bowl. The broth was an uncertain color, and the potatoes had disintegrated. As for meat, I couldn't find any.

"There's no meat in my bowl!" I protested to my friend.

"No meat in mine, either," he replied. "We must have been unlucky."

Later, out in the courtyard, we found out that in fact none of the boys had received any meat. "They lied to us," said one of the boys. "They promised potatoes and meat just to keep us behaving better during the day, the bastards!"

Sometimes we received a few extremely salty olives with our bun. Some of my peers ate the pits of the olives, too. "At least you feel like there's something in your stomach," they argued. A few boys even drank the salty liquid that preserved the olives. They fell ill and spent a night throwing up the paltry contents of their stomachs.

This scrounging mentality was the first sign that hunger was indeed becoming a serious issue in the orphanage. We were simply not getting enough to eat.

There was also a dramatic rise in the number of ill orphans. The clinic had been empty when we had first arrived, but soon there were not enough beds to accommodate all the patients. The orphanage "doctor," who had dubious qualifications, would examine the patients and give them medication. Instead of recovering, many boys died.

Fevzi Bey was not particularly concerned. These poor boys were buried in a small cemetery right outside the orphanage grounds, in extremely shallow graves, where jackals could dig up and desecrate their bodies. What could we do? To whom could we complain?

‿

We gradually learned more about our gilded prison. It had been a monastery, but its previous inhabitants, the monks, had been expelled by the authorities, and Jemal Pasha had taken over a fully functioning institution with a medical clinic, chapel, and dormitories. The small statues that dotted the property and a few large ones on the roof depicted various saints in the act of blessing the faithful. The clock tower in the courtyard looked new and functioned perfectly. The buildings were impressive, and so was the small chapel. It must have been a beautiful retreat from the world.

But now the monastery was filled with hundreds of children, mostly Armenian, in addition to a small contingent of Kurdish orphans. The Kurdish boys and girls initially had shared facilities, but in time they were segregated, just like the Armenian children.

Among a few of the older Armenian boys, Turkishness had begun to take hold. They became the overseers in the classrooms. They carried whips to help keep order both inside the classrooms and outside in the courtyard. They had names like Küçük Enver, Küçük Talaat, Küçük Jemal, Küçük

Hasan.* We were obligated to salute these privileged orphans, just as we were to salute Fevzi Bey. If we failed to salute, we were struck with the whips for our "disrespect."

This was everyday life in the orphanage, a routine occasionally disturbed by an extraordinary event. One of those events occurred soon after our move into the orphanage. A rumor spread among the boys, engendering moments of both fear and joy: apparently, Jemal Pasha was visiting the orphanage to see "his beloved sons" with his own eyes. Supposedly, he was bringing large amounts of food and supplies.

Some of the more imaginative orphans even said his visit might coincide with the Ghurban Bayram, or Feast of Sacrifice,† and he would bring much more than just bread. They predicted he would arrive with fifty or even five hundred sheep to be slaughtered for our benefit.

So when we heard of Jemal Pasha's planned visit, we divided ourselves into two opposing factions. The first faction was made up of the more sanguine boys, who refused to believe that Jemal Pasha would visit "his dear sons" empty-handed. The second faction consisted of the more cynical boys, who had absolutely no faith in this pasha they had never even seen.

On the morning of his visit, teachers and staff members ran about, cleaning the mess hall and sweeping the hallways. In the rush, some of us weren't even allowed to wash ourselves before having to line up at the entrance of our classrooms. The anxious teachers tried their best to enforce harsh discipline. We were told that when he arrived, we should smile and applaud, as well as shout Yaşasin, Jemal Pasha! "Long live Jemal Pasha!"

We waited, standing and sweating profusely in the thick heat, but Jemal Pasha was still nowhere to be seen. We heard the clock tower strike ten. We were exhausted and hungry.

Finally, a large car pulled up to the main gate. A few bodyguards pre-

---

* Küçük means "little." Enver, Talaat, and Jemal were the names of the most prominent Young Turks. These Ottoman officials planned and executed the genocide of the Armenians.

† Known as Eid al-Adha in Arabic, the Ghurban Bayram is an Islamic holiday honoring the willingness of Abraham to sacrifice his first-born son Ishmael, and the latter's assent to be sacrificed, as acts of submission to God's command; God then provided a lamb to be sacrificed instead.

ceded Jemal Pasha. An entire column of military officers followed him. The headmaster and some of the staff obsequiously welcomed the guests at the gate. They all seemed like important people, as they were dressed in clean, fitted uniforms, with sabers swinging from their waist. Jemal Pasha and one other officer had dozens of medals decorating their chests.

Jemal Pasha didn't look particularly impressive: he was of medium height and rather stocky. He had a thin beard, and his cap was pushed down all the way down to his eyes.

In his entourage was a tall, stately lady who walked right behind him. She had a haughty expression in her eyes, and she was exceedingly beautiful. Who was this woman? She reminded me of a relative of mine named Noyemi, who was beautiful and tall like this woman. Noyemi had left our hometown with us, but sometime after reaching the desert outside of Hama, she had died and been buried in the caves.

When Jemal Pasha and his entourage finally reached us, we burst into spasmodic applause and loud cries of *Yaşasin, Jemal Pasha! Yaşasin! Yaşasin!* Fevzi Bey acted very moved by the scene and made only perfunctory gestures to calm us down, as if unable to squelch this spontaneous show of love. The pasha, too, seemed moved by this reception.

But then, just as he was about to inspect our ranks with Fevzi Bey, something unexpected happened: four or five of the older orphans came forward, saluted the pasha respectfully, and bowed. Then one of them spoke in a shaky voice: "Pasha! You are our father! You have saved us from the jaws of death. We will never forget what you have done for us. We were starving to death, and you rescued us. But Pasha, we are still starving! They give us only two tiny buns of bread per day. We are as hungry as we were before we came here, and soon we'll die if you don't help us!"

A huge wave of orphans rushed forward, emboldened, crying out, "We're hungry! We're hungry!" Then, some of the boldest boys ran to the nearby trees, climbed up, and continued the chant, shaking the branches and making a huge racket. Some of them picked the wild fruit off the branches and started eating them.

The pasha was struck dumb. Fevzi Bey was catatonic. Some of the boys who had climbed up the trees fell down. The chaos was getting worse by the minute.

The members of the pasha's entourage furtively glanced at him, waiting for his order. The only woman in the group was crying and wiping her tears with a small handkerchief. Finally, the pasha understood that the longer he stayed, the more likely that he would be exposed to a truly compromising situation. He turned around and gestured to his followers to retreat. They practically tumbled down the stairs leading out of the gate. Fevzi Bey ran after the pasha, apologizing profusely and offering excuses. The pasha and the officers climbed into their cars and drove away, without turning back, but the woman who had come with them stayed behind.

Jemal Pasha had been chased out of the orphanage, beating an abominable retreat. He had been repelled by a bunch of starving boys, whose only crime was that they no longer wanted to be hungry.

Some said that the older boys had gathered a few nights earlier, in the dark, and had plotted this action. Had they thought it through? Had they realized that by appealing to Jemal Pasha's conscience, they were also rebelling against him?

Fevzi Bey's reaction was immediate. That day, eleven o'clock came and went without our getting any food. At five, the mess hall remained closed. Some of the older boys challenged the student küçük beys: "We need to think of these children! They're hungry. They didn't eat at noon. A few people did something stupid, but it's not the kids' fault. They shouldn't have to pay the price!"

The küçük beys made themselves scarce. Confronted with the orphans' rebellion, they had lost their bravado, and throughout that day they refrained from imposing their authority. Eventually, they gathered together and headed to the headmaster's office. At first, they were kept outside the door, but after a few minutes they were admitted.

They stayed in there for quite some time. The headmaster apparently received them coldly, blaming them for the events of the day. They had failed "to prevent a serious breach in order and discipline." The küçük beys promised the headmaster that they would do their utmost to mete out just punishment. "We know how important Jemal Pasha's visit was," they said. "We know, Bey Effendi.* But we've come to ask forgiveness on behalf of the orphans. You are the father figure for all these boys. A father enforces discipline, but also forgives his wayward sons. The younger boys are terribly hungry. They weren't given any food at eleven, and it doesn't look like they'll get any dinner, either. Bey Effendi, their hunger will only cause more disorder. Their lives are in your hands."

Fevzi Bey sent them out with an order to squelch any further rebellion. The küçük beys left, grumbling that the headmaster was always beating children and leaving them hungry. We congregated around them and asked if we would eat before bed.

"There will be no food today," announced Küçük Talaat, to everyone's dismay.

All over the courtyard, in the hallways, and in the bedrooms, boys were gathered in groups, talking about the events of the day, offering their perspectives and analyses while their stomachs rumbled with hunger. Some were curious about the wild fruit that had fallen from the trees, but they were far from edible.

"They're so bitter!" said one boy, spitting a chunk out. "They taste like poison!"

"Don't eat those things! They'll kill you!" said another.

These boys of seven or eight, instead of playing games and horsing around, were discussing issues of life and death.

I was almost tempted to join in their experiments. Usually I received extra pieces of bread from Krikor, which filled up at least a corner of my stomach, but he had not appeared all day. I was starving. I remembered how some of the more optimistic boys had believed that Jemal Pasha was bringing truckloads of bread and sweets for us. Those fantasies had been shattered, and we were left with this sad reality.

The staff had prepared a special meal to be served during Jemal Pasha's visit—pilaf with bulgur. Unfortunately, none of us tasted it that day. We

---

* *Bey effendi* is an honorific equivalent to "mister."

went to bed with empty stomachs. The pilaf was served the next day; we each got a ladle-full, alongside the usual walnut-sized bun.

ᔒ

By this time, the administration had declared full-scale war on the remaining vestiges of our Armenian identities. If we uttered a single Armenian word, we were punished harshly. The entire staff of the orphanage, as well as the thirty or forty guards who were stationed in Antoura, took this ban on the Armenian language very seriously. Though the main tactics employed against us in this war were violence and terror, some staff members did make half-hearted attempts to capture our hearts and minds. A few of the female teachers, especially, tried to act in the most motherly way possible.

"Speak Turkish, boys. Turkish is a beautiful language," they smiled at us. Some of these teachers were young and pretty. But the orphans were aware that underneath their kindness, they were trying to destroy our very selves. Therefore, we had a natural revulsion toward them.

In most classes, we suffered pitiless beatings and severe verbal abuse. The staff's behavior toward us was absolutely barbaric and would have shocked any outside observer. In every classroom the teacher had access to a bunch of canes kept in the back of the room. A *falakha** cane always hung from a nail, next to a thick rope to tie the feet of the guilty boys.

Our classes were Turkish language; catechism and religious history; penmanship; biology and zoology; music and singing; and physical education. But how were we to become educated, erudite men in an atmosphere of such utter oppression?

Physical education was the simplest of the classes. There were no calisthenics and no organized games. We were simply made to march, like soldiers, for an hour and a half. The teacher was an old soldier, a coarse and vulgar man, ready to rain down blows on any boy for the slightest infraction. Like many of the other teachers, if his victim fell to the ground, he kicked him in the face and the ribs. He often knocked out my peers' teeth.

---

* A cane or strap used to strike the soles of the feet, also known as a bastinado, falanga, and falaka. In the modern world, its use is considered a form of torture.

Mullah Nejmeddin taught us catechism and religious history. He was tall, wide-shouldered, with gray hair and a gray beard, and he always wore a red fez. An extremely violent and venal man, he understood the principles of bribery and the baseness to which we lowered ourselves when food was concerned. He kept his pockets full of small bread buns. We couldn't understand a word he said, but whenever he asked *Anladınız mı?* "Do you understand me?," we responded "Yes, teacher, sir!" In response, he would murmur *afferin*, "good job," and reward us with an extra bun.

Our Turkish language teacher was Nabiheh Khanum, a buxom, healthy woman around forty years old, with a friendly disposition—though that facade of kindness quickly faded when she was irritated. Then she would beat us. After an entire year, she was barely able to teach us a few Turkish words.

In Nabiheh Khanum's class, we learned mostly vocabulary, simple phrases, and the simple tenses. We constantly repeated phrases such as: "I eat bread, I ate bread, I will eat bread . . . I drink water, I drank water, I will drink water . . ."

One of the boys dared step out of line. "Miss!" he called out. "We can't eat bread because there is none!"

"Which one of you dared say that?" she screamed. "What gall!" She waved a stick above our heads. Boys dodged out of her way as she charged down the rows of desks. For some reason, she fixated on Apraham in the second row, and she began striking him. But Apraham, an older boy, refused to accept the beating. Instead, he lunged at the teacher, responding to the blows of her stick with his fists. The other boys made a deafening din.

Fevzi Bey appeared in the doorway. "All of you! Sit down!" he yelled.

Apraham, bleeding from the nose, stared down the headmaster and spat out: "Sir, we are hungry! All these boys are hungry!"

Fevzi Bey advanced on Apraham, lifted him off his feet, and threw him backwards onto the floor. We hunched down in our seats, while the headmaster stood over Apraham's limp body, staring daggers at the rest of us, waiting to pounce if he heard a single peep.

The bell rang, announcing the beginning of recess. It always rang on schedule. It kept ringing, but as long as the headmaster was there, no one moved. The teacher, meanwhile, gathered her things and crept out of the room, blushing with embarrassment and trying to cover her torn dress.

Fevzi Bey nudged Apraham in the ribs with the tip of his shoe. Apraham moved. He was not dead, at least.

"Get on your feet! Now!" ordered Fevzi Bey. Apraham remained motionless. "Get up!" repeated the headmaster.

Students gathered outside the door, curious to see what the commotion was all about.

The headmaster once again repeated his order. Apraham tried to stand up, but couldn't. The headmaster grabbed him roughly by the arm, pulled him to his feet, and shook him. "Walk!" he barked.

The headmaster dragged Apraham out into the courtyard. We all ran after them, curious to watch the next episode of this unfolding tragedy.

By the time we reached the courtyard, the bell rang again, marking the end of recess. It sounded like a desperate appeal to Fevzi Bey to spare the unfortunate Apraham. But the headmaster kept dragging him away. As we walked back to our classroom, we feared for our friend.

In science class, we couldn't care less about the difference between vertebrate and invertebrate animals. All of our thoughts were with Apraham. The teacher futilely tried to focus our attention by banging her large wooden ruler on her table, but our minds wandered. We didn't misbehave. We didn't even think of our hunger pangs or the tasteless potato soup. We just waited for the bell so we could run outside and check on our classmate.

As soon as the bell rang, we poured out of the classroom. Apraham had been made to stand in the searing sun. He was sweating profusely and clearly still hurting from his beating. A guard carrying a large stick stood beside him. Apraham had to stand in the direct sunlight until dusk.

The next day, he had to stand in the sun again. On the third day, he did the same. It was a new form of torture conceived by Fevzi Bey. During our recesses and after our meals, we would run to Apraham, who was always there, standing next to the menacing guard, tears running down his cheeks. They had broken him physically, and they had broken his pride. Despite all our prayers, the sun never moved any faster, though eventually, it would slide beneath the horizon, and Apraham's torture could end. After three days, the poor boy was utterly destroyed.

Another time, a teacher overheard two boys mock a chant of the Ottoman army. "Say that again you bastards! Say that again!" he screamed. Blows of his stick rained upon the poor boys, landing on their shoulders, backs, ribs, and even heads. When they fell to the ground, the teacher pounced on them and began kicking them. The two boys were huddled on the floor, in the fetal position, bleeding heavily.

By the time the bell rang and we saw the spectacle, the teacher had left the scene, unwilling to face hundreds of orphans with what he had done.

Fevzi Bey knew that the wave of discontent was reaching a new crest. He intended to prevent more rebellion by nipping all dissatisfaction in the bud. He installed new guidelines, which were meant to instill terror in the orphans.

Every evening, right before sunset, we gathered in the middle of the courtyard. There, we would have to salute the Turkish flag as it was lowered and call out *Yaşasin! Yaşasin, Jemal Pasha!* at the top of our lungs. This was another way of Turkifying us, of course.

Now, after the flag ceremony, Fevzi Bey mounted the improvised stage with a piece of paper. Behind him were all the tools of falakha torture— canes, staffs, ropes, and buckets of water. Calmly, as if reading a shopping list, he called out the names of the boys who would receive corporal punishment.

He had general guidelines for the punishments we received, according to the severity of our transgressions. Those who were found guilty of theft, who fought teachers or guards, or who caused disorder in the courtyard would receive between twenty-five and one hundred strokes of the falakha, depending on their age. Those who disrespected Islam, the Turkish language, or the Turkish nation, as well as those who spoke Armenian, prayed in Armenian, or made the sign of the cross, could receive up to two hundred strokes of the falakha, or even three hundred in particularly egregious cases, provided that halfway through the guards would pause and douse the victim's feet with cold water.

He started with the youngest ones. One child was found guilty of speaking Armenian and was condemned to twenty-five strokes. Two guards tied his feet together, lifted him up into the air upside down, and presented the soles of his bare feet to Fevzi Bey, who picked up the falakha cane and hit the boy with sadistic pleasure. The boy screamed in pain and cried for his mother. Eventually the pain was too much, and he fainted. He was carried off to the clinic.

Two other boys, also around the age of seven, were punished with twenty-five strokes for the same crime. They too were eventually carried off to the clinic.

Then a boy of about ten was called up. He received fifty strokes for having dared use his mother tongue, and he, too, was taken to the clinic.

He was followed by a twelve-year-old boy who was found guilty of having insulted the Turkish nation or language. He was struck one hundred times. He had to be doused with water, and he woke up some time later in the clinic.

Four or five older boys had been accused of disobeying Mullah Nejmeddin and insulting Islam. After receiving two hundred strokes each, they looked dead. It was hard to believe they were still breathing.

The entire spectacle was watched by over a thousand people—the entire student body and faculty of the orphanage.

Many of the punished boys couldn't walk for weeks. Some lost their teeth and broke their noses. Most fainted while crying for mercy or pathetically screaming for their mothers.

This was a daily event for two years, and all of us headed to the flag-lowering ceremony shaking with terror. Though not all were beaten, all were punished—we all were humiliated, reminded that being Armenian was a punishable crime.

Fevzi Bey always delivered the first blow. Only when he tired did the guards take over. They were just as ruthless as the headmaster. They were all convinced that the condemned students had committed serious infractions, although the boys' only fault was that they couldn't speak Turkish and had to use their native tongue to communicate. Sometimes we didn't know how our crimes had been discovered, and rumors ran rampant that there were informers among us.

My mother had never taught me a single word in Turkish; she had never seen the need. I spent much of my time in solitude, though I was not shy and I enjoyed interacting with others. I mostly kept myself mute out of fear that an Armenian word would slip out of my lips. I spoke only when I was among trusted friends. This way, I thought I would escape the falakha. I was soon proven wrong. One evening, my name was read. I had been betrayed! Two boys were alongside me. I was not yet six years old.

After the first few strikes, I cried out in pain, and then I blacked out—I don't remember a thing. I don't even remember how many times I was hit. When I opened my eyes, I realized I was lying in a bed in the clinic, alongside the two other boys who had shared my fate.

The next morning, Krikor paid me a visit. He told me how I had been beaten, how I had screamed in pain, and how he had almost attacked the Turkish guards to come to my rescue. He wanted to rub my feet, but I didn't let him. Every time he touched them, I screamed in pain. He stayed for a while, chatted with me, and tried to lift my spirits. Right before taking his leave, he slipped two extra buns of bread under my pillow and embraced me.

The two boys who had been punished with me soon limped toward my bed. We stared at each other's feet and faces in horror, knowing we presented similar spectacles. I split the two buns into three equal shares, and we ate. Then, as our moods slightly brightened, we chatted for a few minutes in Armenian.

About ten days later, a nurse came around, examined our feet, made us walk a few steps, and dismissed us from the clinic. We didn't understand a word she said, but we realized that we now had to return to our regular routine.

We came out into the courtyard. It was a pleasant, sunny day. The orphans were playing in the shade of the trees.

I saw Halide Edip Adıvar,* the woman who had stayed behind after Jemal Pasha's visit. She would often lean against the sundial and watch us

---

* Halide Edip Adıvar was a prominent novelist and educator associated with the causes of women's rights and Turkish nationalism. During the Great War she served for a time as an Ottoman inspector of schools.

play. She seemed carefree. Sometimes she journeyed to Beirut and returned a few days later with stacks of books under her arms. Some said that she was writing a book about the orphans; others claimed that at night, she sucked the blood out of the necks of the older boys. We didn't know what to believe. Did she think of our suffering? Did she think of our terrible pasts or our bleak futures? Did she have any motherly instincts that allowed her to sympathize with us? Whenever the bell rang to rush us into our classrooms, she would go into her quarters and stay there until the evening, when she reappeared for the flag-lowering ceremony and the beatings that followed.

As the weeks passed, the number of the boys being punished stayed consistent, but the nature of their infractions changed. Fewer and fewer orphans were found guilty of speaking Armenian. Fevzi Bey and his cronies considered this a great victory. However, the number of boys accused of theft was on the rise. The stolen goods were always food—from the storerooms or the mess hall, as well as from the vegetable gardens. Some even stole delicacies and fruit from the teachers' lounge and from other staff offices, and others slipped beyond the orphanage's walls to scavenge for food.

The boys were pitilessly subjected to the falakha when caught stealing, but they were so hungry, and so in love with life, that even the menace of the beatings could not discourage them from taking the risk. This was a battle against death.

The pangs of hunger were so terrible that some boys resorted to desperate measures—they ate paper, drank ink, and swallowed dead flies that they found around the courtyard. We were basically becoming feral, performing acts that would have nauseated us when we were still back home with our families. For two years we lived like this. The youngest of the boys in the orphanage were about my age. We had spent two formative years in hunger, misery, fear, and pain, and we had become disillusioned, cynical, and emaciated. But we had not yielded a single inch. We had kept our faith, our language, and our identities intact.

∽

Rumors began circulating that Fevzi Bey was going to leave the orphanage. We breathed a sigh of relief, looking forward to the imminent end of our collective nightmare.

Yet Fevzi Bey grew only more brutal. He vented his anger on the orphans every evening. Two boys, Manuel and Mgrdich, were sentenced to three hundred strokes of the falakha, in three rounds, for desecrating the Turkish flag. As usual, Fevzi Bey chose the sturdiest cane and brutally attacked the soles of their feet. But after fifty strokes he began panting and relinquished the privilege of torturing the children to the soldier standing closest to him, who seemed to want to outdo Fevzi Bey. By that time, the boys had already fainted, but the punishment continued.

Eventually, their limp bodies were dragged off to the clinic. Neither the teachers nor the staff members—not even Halide Edip—batted an eyelid at this display of savagery. By then it was dark, and we were told to retire to our dormitories, which remained deadly silent all night, though none of us slept.

I lay in bed for hours. Softly, under my breath, I recited the Hayr Mer and bits and pieces of any other prayers I could remember. The image of Manuel and Mgrdich fainting under the beating kept coming back to me. Manuel was actually a distant relative of mine, and Mgrdich had been a neighbor of ours in Tsakh Tsor. I begged God to preserve their lives and heal them as quickly as possible.

At dawn, we went into the courtyard. It was another beautiful day. The rising sun portended a warm day, and the birds flitted about from tree to tree, filling the air with their chorus.

One of the caretakers approached the orphans and whispered: "He's leaving."

"Who's leaving?" asked one of the boys.

She replied: *Fevzi Bey—dinsiz, imansız*. "Fevzi Bey—infidel, faithless."

"Fevzi Bey is leaving! Fevzi Bey is leaving!" The excitement sent us off in all directions. We delivered the good news to anyone we came across.

The brutal falakha ceremony involving Manuel and Mgrdich had been his parting shot. He would no longer haunt us. A few guards loaded his baggage into a waiting carriage, and within minutes he came out of his office, mounted the carriage without turning back or saying a word, and forever exited the orphanage and our lives.

Not a single teacher bade him farewell. The troops didn't even salute him. He left with his tail between his legs, like a king who had been forced to abdicate. Why? What had he done to anger the relevant authorities? Nobody knew.

That entire day, whether in the classroom or in the courtyard, we boldly spoke Armenian. We had scored our first substantial victory in our battle against the forces of Turkification.

CHAPTER 6

THE RAIDS

SOON AFTER FEVZI BEY'S DEPARTURE, Krikor handed me a few extra buns of bread and announced that he was leaving the orphanage. He wasn't escaping hunger or disease—he was one of the best-fed and healthiest boys in the institution. But his longing for his family was tearing him apart. He had decided to rejoin them in the camp outside Hama.

He cried as he left me. He hated the idea of leaving me behind.

"Tell your mother and Ardashes that . . ." I began, but I couldn't continue. I burst into tears.

During the night Krikor climbed over the wall and disappeared into the nearby woods. He never returned.

Others had escaped before Krikor. Despite warnings that attempted escapes would be punished severely, orphans had tried to leave on a regular basis. Many must have succeeded, but we also heard stories of those shot to death by the guards or residents of Antoura. Either way, those who escaped had no means of informing us of their fate. They simply disappeared into the darkness.

Krikor had been my closest friend and protector. After his departure, I was alone and vulnerable. I had friends my own age with whom I played in the courtyard and endured punishments such as the falakha, but I had yet to develop an intimate, close friendship with any of them. Then, one day my friend Mihran whispered to me, "Why don't you join our group?"

"What group?" I asked.

"Once you join, you'll know," he replied mysteriously.

"What do you guys do?" I persisted.

"I'll tell you one thing—we're never hungry," he answered.

I brooded over Mihran's words all day. Since Krikor's escape, I had been hungrier than ever, deprived of that extra bread. A few days later, I found myself alone with Mihran and I broached the topic.

"So, what kind of group were you talking about the other day?" I asked.

"We'll be going on a raid tonight," he replied. "I'll wake you up and you'll come with us."

"Where will we be going?"

"We're going to steal food. Don't worry, we won't be going outside the walls, we'll just be visiting the mess hall, the kitchen, and the storerooms."

"And then?"

"Then? We'll fill our bags with whatever food we find."

"How are we going to sneak in? What if we get caught?"

"Don't worry about that."

All day I waited with impatience and trepidation. Within a few hours I would officially become a thief. I almost regretted getting myself involved.

During class, I couldn't concentrate. I feared that if we got caught, we would be punished and branded as thieves forever. After dinner, while the others played, I retired to a corner and lost myself in thought. In the distance, leaning against the clock tower, was Halide Edip, watching the children, smiling as she heard Turkish from many of them.

The new headmaster was Mukhtar Bey—another Turk, but a very different kind of man. On the first evening of his arrival, a few hours before my first adventure with Mihran and his friends, we held the flag-lowering ceremony, after which we were promptly told to disperse. For the first time in two years, there were no punishments, no falakha. Those horrid devices of torture had seen their last day in the Antoura orphanage.

At night, most of the orphans slept better than they had for two years. But not me. I pulled the sheet over my head, whispered the Hayr Mer, crossed myself, and tried to sleep, but premonitions of doom kept racing through my mind. Mukhtar Bey seemed like a kind man. Was it worth antagonizing him on the night of his arrival? Was it not better to call off the raid?

Mihran slept only a couple of beds away from me, and he had promised to wake me up at the right time. He had ordered me to follow him silently and without hesitation. All kinds of doubts crept into my thoughts. Why should I steal? After all, I was already accustomed to hunger. But I had given Mihran my word, and I felt trapped by that promise.

At some point I must have dozed off. I don't know how long I slept before I was woken up by a soft touch. I got to my feet and followed Mihran out of the room. We went down the stairs and met a few boys who were hiding in the shadows. Their Armenian names were Nishan, Boghos, and Kalust. I knew them all from the Hama orphanage. It was clear that the team's leader was Mihran; he was by far the oldest. Each boy carried a bag, and I was handed one, too.

We crossed ourselves and advanced toward the kitchen and storeroom, located in an adjacent building. The door was locked. Then we went to a window. From the inside, we could hear the shuffle of feet and whispers of conversation. When we climbed through the window, we came face-to-face with another team of boys on the prowl for food. We all knew each other, and there was no need for idle talk. Without saying anything, they nodded to us and left through the same window we had come through. Now alone, we began looking for something to steal. Though a sliver of light seeped in through the windows, the darkness was impenetrable. We shuffled about, banging into things and looking for anything edible. Finally, we found bags of potatoes, along with some garlic and onions. Deep inside the cabinets we found lentils, chickpeas, and beans.

God must have been watching over us, for we were able to escape the building unnoticed. We went back into the dorm, where all was silent. Now, in the dark, we had to find our beds. Before retiring, we handed everything we had gathered to Mihran and Boghos. They knew where to hide it all. Then we climbed into our beds, satisfied with our success. There were still some hours before dawn.

As I pulled the sheet over me, I breathed a sigh of relief. Our nocturnal adventure had not been as terrifying as I had expected, especially considering the large amount of supplies we had netted. The immediate future promised to be free from hunger.

The next morning, I joined my co-conspirators in an isolated corner of the courtyard where Mihran filled our pockets with handfuls of chickpeas. He reminded us not to eat in front of other boys. So we had to hide in the shadows and eat the chickpeas one by one. The next day we ate the lentils, then the beans, and so on. Raw chickpeas were tolerable, but the lentils and beans tasted terrible. I think it took us two entire weeks to eat through the supplies we had stolen during the raid.

"There are dozens of small groups like ours," Mihran told me.

"Do they all get their food from the storeroom?" I asked.

"If you pay attention to exactly what they're eating, you'll know where they got it from. If not the storeroom, they get vegetables and fruit from the garden," he replied. "Sometimes they switch targets."

"Will we go to the vegetable garden, too?"

"When the time comes, I'll let you know."

"But again, what if we get caught?"

"Whatever happens, we'll keep doing what we do. We're not thieves; we're simply trying to survive. There's no other way."

Mihran was only ten years old, but he acted like an adult. He was willful, bold, and enterprising. The more I thought of Mihran, the more his stature grew in my eyes. This boy, who looked like so many others wearing the gray orphanage uniform, possessed not only rare courage, but also the willingness to lead others.

Mukhtar Bey didn't last long as headmaster, mainly because he was an actual human being. He couldn't bear the sight of emaciated orphans or the disregard of the authorities who were responsible for them. Despite his urgent appeals, the supplies sent out to the orphanage remained abysmally meager, and he could do nothing to improve our quality of life. He had been told that the government could spare nothing more.

The clinic was no longer filled with boys who had been beaten black and blue by the falakha, but by boys who suffered from all kinds of ailments. Given the lack of competent doctors or nurses, not a week passed without one or two orphans dying in the clinic's beds. Those boys were buried with the others, right outside the walls in shallow graves.

One evening, Mihran came to me and whispered, "We go again tonight."

"To the storeroom again?"

"We'll see," he replied before walking away.

That night, when I climbed into bed, I crossed myself and said my prayers with a calm heart. I now trusted Mihran and no longer tormented myself with thoughts of what would happen if we were caught.

It was past midnight when Mihran woke me up. I followed in his foot-steps. We roused Boghos and Kalust and crept down the stairs.

This time, we didn't head toward the kitchen and storeroom. As we passed by the small chapel, I crossed myself and continued on. We then faced the wall that separated the courtyard of the orphanage from the outside world. It wasn't particularly tall, and there was no guard in sight. We climbed up, then jumped down into the free world. We immediately found ourselves in thick woods. Creeping through the underbrush, we reached the vegetable garden. Fortunately, there were still no guards in sight—they had probably abandoned their posts and were sleeping.

Mihran immediately gave us our tasks. My job was to gather cucum-bers, Boghos was to pick green beans, Kalust was to dig up potatoes, and Mihran decided to gather some fruit from the nearby trees. We had to return to our dorms within minutes—and with our bags full.

In the opaque darkness of the night, I dropped to my knees and stumbled upon a bush. I picked a large cucumber and moved on. Within minutes, my bag was virtually full. I picked one last cucumber and eagerly bit into it. It was fresh and juicy, like nothing I had eaten for months. My mother had always told us to wash vegetables before we ate them, but those days were long past. The only thing I cared about at the moment was the taste of life in my mouth.

We were leaving the vegetable garden, carrying our bulging bags over our shoulders, when we heard the crowing of some roosters and the baying of distant hounds. We had to hurry. We climbed over the wall, helping each other, and jumped into the courtyard. As we passed the chapel, Kalust and I handed our bags to Boghos, who followed Mihran while we rushed to our dormitory and snuck into our beds.

The next day, during recess, Mihran stealthily slipped a cucumber into each of our pockets. The recess was short and I didn't have the time to eat it before the bell rang. During class, I occasionally touched it and salivated madly. My patience was tested to the limits. I couldn't concentrate on anything the teacher said.

As soon as the bell rang for the next recess, I ran behind a column in the courtyard and devoured the cucumber. Then I wiped my mouth and ran to my friends, feeling terribly guilty for having eaten it by myself. I could have shared it with several of these unfortunate boys.

The cucumbers were finished within a few days. We moved on to carrots, and then to green beans. The carrots were delicious, but the raw beans were barely edible. What could we do? We just gulped them down with water.

Within two weeks we exhausted our supply of vegetables and began planning our next raid. The easiest, most logical targets were the storeroom and the kitchen. Meanwhile, Mihran and the leaders of the other clandestine teams had decided to coordinate all actions, so that different teams would not target the same area on the same night. If two teams decided to raid the storerooms simultaneously, they would have to leave the area and stick to theirs, regardless of the quantity and quality of their booty.

In a few days, Mihran woke me up as usual, and we met up with the other members of our team.

"We'll be raiding the storeroom again," Mihran announced authoritatively and took off. We followed him with blind obedience. Within a few minutes, we were at the familiar window. But this time the window was secured from the inside with metal bars. The orphanage authorities finally had noticed that the bags of supplies were getting lighter every night.

We ran to the other side of the building to try the other windows, but they were all barred. However, there was an opening at the very top of them through which we could jump down into the storeroom. Somehow, Mihran was able to reach this opening and jump through, astounding us with his agility. While we waited for what seemed like hours, every sound was magnified and seemed like a guard running toward us.

"He's late," commented Kalust anxiously.

"He's *very* late. The sun's about to rise," added Boghos.

"Mihran knows what he's doing," I tried to reassure them and myself.

He certainly did. Soon we heard muffled shuffling from inside, then the unmistakable sound of someone climbing up the wall. Mihran's head popped out from the opening at the top of the window. With some difficulty, he swung a heavy bag over his shoulder and dangled it down to us. Boghos grabbed it. Mihran disappeared back inside and repeated the sequence with another bag. Then he somehow climbed back out of the opening, swung his legs down while still holding on to the ledge, then jumped down. He was sweating profusely and breathing heavily.

"We've got no time to rest. Let's go!" he ordered. We bolted.

As we retreated back to the dormitories, we came face to face with another team of boys who were out on a raid and were advancing toward the storeroom.

Our two bags contained chickpeas. Mihran took them to the hideout while we crept into our beds.

Two bags of chickpeas. Much less than I had expected, but better than nothing. For a couple of weeks we would have to force them down our throats, until we ate them all and organized another raid.

Mihran had become an expert at slipping handfuls of these chickpeas into our pockets. To others, it truly looked like he was simply running into us for only a fraction of a second. We, too, had to eat very stealthily. The chickpeas were dry and hard. I was afraid I would break my teeth.

After two weeks of chickpeas, Mihran again whispered, "We go tonight." His orders were always concise, precise, and incontrovertible. He was almost like a machine that was always wound, an unemotional robot.

Late that night, we all met up and went downstairs. We climbed over the wall and ran into the vegetable garden, which seemed so inviting in the silvery moonlight. Suddenly, we heard screams and sounds of struggle from nearby. Mihran, showing his true colors, ran toward the commotion. Rallied by his example, we followed in his tracks.

When we arrived, the scene before us was scarcely believable—a few of the older orphans were battering a guard. They had taken the man's pistol and were beating him senseless. One of the boys was sitting on his chest, raining down blows. Eventually, they tied the guard's legs together and threatened to kill him with the pistol if he didn't stop struggling. Under Mihran's command, we joined forces with these boys.

As the guard cowered, we filled our bags with cucumbers, tomatoes, carrots, and potatoes. Our work was done. Taking the guard's pistol with us, we headed for the wall.

We left the gun outside, under the wall, and snuck inside. Mihran collected all of our bags, and we slipped into our beds.

A bunch of boys had defeated a soldier of the mighty Ottoman army! They had even taken his gun and discarded it as if it were useless. As I curled up in bed that night, I reflected that it was probably the most otherworldly scene I had ever witnessed.

The next morning, as we headed for lunch, Kalust whispered in my ear: "Forget the afternoon classes. We're going to go grind bones."

The boys who stole vegetables from the fields sometimes brought back the bones of other dead orphans, which the jackals dug up from the shallow graves. The boys ground them into a powder and drank it with water.

Our hunger made us desperate, and it dehumanized us. I didn't feel much revulsion at the idea. All we thought of was food, and this was yet another way to fight hunger.

In the afternoon, Kalust and I met with three boys named Kevork, Nishan, and Arshag behind the chapel. Supposedly, all three were experts at handling bones.

Some cobblestones covered the ground right underneath the walls. The boys dislodged one of them to use as an anvil. They also gathered some very large rocks for ersatz hammers. Then, they found bits and pieces of human bones underneath the rocks outside the walls. Now they set to work, bashing the bones with the rocks. They did so again and again, until the bones were crushed into a fine powder. The actual process took almost three hours, and the three experts were exhausted by the labor.

It was unpleasant, but what could I do? I pulled back my sleeves and set to work with ardor. I tried my best to help the others. The most difficult part was finding the bones to crush. We had to go outside the perimeter of the orphanage and look for them under rocks. We often didn't know what kinds of bones we were taking back to the others, nor did we bother to figure it out. We had sunk *that* low.

One day, soon afterward, we were looking for bones outside the fence. We were so absorbed in our work that we failed to notice the approach of Mullah Nejmeddin.

"What are you doing out here?"

"We're finding bones to turn into powder, so we'll feel less hungry," answered Arshag.

"Don't they give you enough work? Must you desecrate the dead?"

"The food is not enough. If it were, we obviously would never do this," replied Arshag.

"Sir, we don't want to starve to death. We want to live. What can we do? We've got to eat what we find," added Nishan.

The mullah, utterly shocked, shook his head and walked away. This same man satisfied his rotund belly not only with the meals given to him and other staff, but also with the additional bread (sometimes thirty or forty buns of it) that he took to his room every evening after dinner. We had seen him walk to his bedroom with a basket full of these buns. Sometimes, the boys would pretend to be running about when he reached the bottom of the stairs that led to his quarters, and one of them would bump into him, upsetting the basket, allowing the others to surreptitiously collect any buns that fell to the floor.

During Fevzi Bey's tenure, anyone caught stealing would have to submit to the falakha. Now, boys caught stealing food were punished by having to remain in the classrooms during recess for three to six days, or by having to stand and watch friends play during recess, without being able to participate in their games. Ever since the punishment softened, theft rose.

As the administration increased surveillance around the storerooms, kitchen, and vegetable garden, we had to raid farther away from the orphanage to find our loot.

The closest home to the orphanage was one we called "the small house." Only one man lived in it, with his two sheep and several hens. Another home close to the wall was called "the big house," and it was inhabited by an elderly couple. They had a barn in one corner of their property, from which we often heard the mooing of a cow. Both homes also had orchards, but the biggest one belonged to a priest called Father Francis—his land was full of fruit-bearing trees and vegetables.

One night, we climbed over the wall and ran into the woods that surrounded the orphanage. After advancing about a hundred meters, we passed out of the woods and by the orphanage cemetery. The ground was littered with skeletons and loose bones, and the jackals feasted upon them, filling the air with their baying. I crossed that area without a great sensation of terror and dread.

We eventually reached the gardens and orchards of the orphanage's neighbors, and as we filled our bags, I buried my morbid thoughts of the cemetery. In those days at Antoura, it was so easy to die, and so hard to survive.

❧

At night, elderly Turkish women patrolled up and down the rows of beds, trying their best to make sure we were all asleep. Some of us slept four to a bed, others eight to a bed, covered by one single blanket, breathing into each other's faces. On cold nights, boys sometimes pulled the blanket off the others, starting an argument. The commotion would wake up everyone in the dormitory, and the women would do their best to restore order.

Often, the boys cried out in their sleep, or they woke up from a nightmare. When that happened, the Turkish women took their hands, escorted them to the lavatories, washed away their tears, and brought them back to the beds.

I often dreamed of my mother. During these dreams, we had long conversations. I was told that I often whimpered and repeated the word "mother" in my sleep. Her nightly visits were essential to my sanity and survival.

Also, like many of the boys, I would get under the covers, cross myself, and murmur prayers in Armenian. I whispered the Hayr Mer every night, just as my mother had taught me. I barely understood the words, but without any family left, this prayer was basically my only connection to my past and my identity. It was my shield against Turkification.

When morning came, we couldn't help but feel a little bit cheerful. The days were often bright, and out the windows we could see the peaks of mountains in the distance to the east. To the west, in the distance, was the glittering Mediterranean Sea. Around the orphanage were scenic greenery and the beautiful songs of the birds. Despite everything, we had not given up on life yet.

Another thing that lifted our spirits was the set of statues of saints located high on the roofs of the buildings; they seemed to be constantly blessing us, and they were an important reminder of our Christian faith. The orphanage had been Turkified, but this place had been a religious school for decades, and even the Turks could not erase every trace of its past. We felt like those statues had successfully fought off any attempts by the Turks to change their identities, and thus, every time we went out to the courtyard, our eyes were drawn to them.

One morning, we heard a terrible noise, and we saw that the Turks were finally destroying the statues. The saints had lost their battle against the orphanage administration. One of the boys dared ask Mullah Nejmeddin why the saints were being taken away. This infuriated the teacher, who leapt on the boy and beat him with a stick and his fists.

It was difficult to destroy the statues. By the second day only a few of them had been removed. We saw two of them crash down into the courtyard and shatter into a million pieces. That day, every time the bell rang, we poured out of the classrooms and ran to the shattered pieces, picking them up and fretting about them as if they were true relics of the saints.

"I'll miss them," murmured one of the boys.

"They were so lifelike," added another.

"One of them looked exactly like my grandfather—same height, same mustache," said a third, picking up some of the rubble.

The boys kept circling the smashed statues. Nobody played in the courtyard that day. We found noses and ears, arms and legs, scattered all over the place. Mindless destruction. The orphanage staff didn't even bother cleaning up the rubble—the orphans had to collect it all into pails and dispose of it outside the orphanage walls.

Only one statue survived. It was a heavy one, made of bronze, and stood on the altar of the small chapel. But the door of the chapel was always kept locked, so we had no chance of seeing it.

In the first days of our stay in Antoura, the chapel had been a consolation. In the winter it was warm, and in the summer it was cool and breezy. The stained glass windows, decorated with biblical scenes and likenesses of saints, kindled memories of home in our minds.

But the project of Turkification was reaching a new level of intensity. On a daily basis, we heard lectures about Islam, its victories, and the virtue it imparted to the faithful who followed the way of Allah. Some of the boys had succumbed to the pressure already, while the others were under constant assault from the staff and the headmaster.

The administration started locking the chapel doors. It saw the building as a threat to its mission to convert us to Islam.

The orphans cast furtive glances toward the locked doors. "When will they let us back into the chapel?" asked one boy.

"To pray? We can pray anywhere," answered another. "Remember, boys, we can pray in our beds, in our rooms, or even here in the courtyard."

"I know that, but I wish I could see the statues inside one more time," a third added.

"We can't break down the door, but there are other ways to get in," insisted a boy named Murad. "I'll find a way and I'll let you in, just follow me!"

The bell rang. It was the end of recess, and we had to return to the classrooms. We formed rows and walked into class under the watchful gaze of the teachers. During history class, the teacher asked whether Muhammad traveled on the back of a camel or on the back of a donkey. One of the more daring boys stood up and replied: "Miss, we all know Muhammad traveled on the back of a camel, and he must have really struck a sorry figure. As for those statues, they were beautiful. What was the point of smashing them to pieces?"

The entire class burst into laughter.

"How dare you? What blasphemy!" cried out the teacher, and struck her desk with her ruler.

For the crime of insulting the prophet, the boy had to face the wall and stand on one leg until the end of the class. But the classroom was now out of control, with all the students making a terrible amount of noise.

That night, Murad, as promised, led a group toward the back of the chapel. There we found a tiny door that was unlocked. Once through it, we found ourselves in a secondary room full of drawers, closets, and other furniture, covered by a thick layer of dust. But that didn't interest us. We crept into the main nave. It was completely dark, save for a glimmer of light peeking through the window. As we approached the altar, we spotted the statue—it was lying on the ground, on its back.

The Turks had managed to dislodge it from its plinth, but they had failed to destroy it. It had only a few nicks here and there. The metallic statue had been too strong for their hammers and anvils. The serene expression on the statue's face was still the same. In the visage of this statue we found more beauty and dignity than ever.

We all sat solemnly around the fallen statue. There was a silent, holy conversation going on between it and us. We weren't even quite sure who the statue was supposed to depict. But we knew it was another link to our pasts, another key to our memories.

∾

It was getting more difficult to go on our raids outside the perimeter of the orphanage. Father Francis, tired of being robbed, got a rifle and a dog to protect his property. The dog was huge and looked like a wolf—it spent the nights barking and baying, keeping everyone awake and instilling terror in the hearts of the orphans on raiding parties.

The "small house" and the "big house" fell on tough times. Hunger was spreading across the villages of the area. These elderly people's children had left for other parts of the country to find food. They were on the edge of starvation now, living only on their vegetables and fruit.

One time, we climbed over the wall and headed for the garden of the "small house." We saw no lights from the house. Our leader climbed over the short fence, but as soon as he jumped down, Father Francis's dog started barking, waking the old man and bringing him to the balcony. Our leader jumped back to the other side, and after a short consultation we had to flee. The dog had awakened the entire village.

By this time I had joined a new group led by Yusuf, a bold and serious boy. "Follow me!" he said. "I know the house of a villager nearby with a small orchard!"

There was nobody inside the house. Yusuf said the owner had gone to a city to find bread. The famine had reached his door.

How did Yusuf know all this? There was no time to ask. Stumbling in the undergrowth, we followed in his tracks. In the orchard, silence and darkness surrounded us. We tried to find some fruit, but to no avail. We couldn't even distinguish the different types of trees in the darkness.

We gave up on the trees and tried to find something in the bushes. We found a few lonely pumpkins and some dried-out tomatoes, eggplants, and beans. We stuffed our loot into our pockets. Then we found some small potatoes and onions as we dug into the soil. It was a poor result, but after an hour of searching, it was all we could find.

It was almost dawn. In the distance, we heard the crowing of the roosters and the barking of Father Francis's dog. Our team reached the orphanage wall, but we heard sounds of conversation from the other side. So we went around the wall, to the back of the chapel, and climbed over the wall there. This was not an easy task, but Yusuf helped us all get across.

We tiptoed to our dormitories. I snuck into my bed and got under the blanket. The other boys didn't even stir.

"Mamma, Mamma," whimpered someone from nearby in his sleep. It had been two years, yet the boy still called for his mother, who was probably long dead.

The ringing of the bell soon roused me. Along with the other boys I left the dormitory, trying to shake off my drowsiness.

In the courtyard, Yusuf signaled to our team to gather in the corner. We were experienced in these matters by now, and we left the mass of orphans one by one, in order not to draw attention to our movements.

Once we were alone, Yusuf extracted some plums and a few dried-out tomatoes from his pockets. "Eat up," he said. "They're not very ripe, but they'll help you forget about your hunger."

We had to wait another three hours until breakfast. We each went our separate ways and stealthily ate the bitter tomatoes, which tasted horrible. Soon the bell rang again, and we waited in line to enter our classrooms, ready to begin another day filled with insults and beatings from cruel teachers, with meals of tiny buns and bland, colorless gruel of a suspicious origin.

The targets of our food raids—the storerooms and the vegetable gardens—had been exhausted. The administration had increased its surveillance, and Father Francis's dog was always making a racket. Some boys had even disappeared lately—perhaps they had been killed by that dog.

We had become scavengers and thieves, putting life and limb in danger for a few scraps. Yet we had to survive.

Yusuf led another raid that night. In the moonlight, we tiptoed down the stairs, but instead of heading toward the chapel, we went toward the gymnasium; the area was not usually patrolled by too many guards.

Once over the wall, we found ourselves in a thicket, walking through thorny bushes. We traced a curve in the woods and once again found ourselves in the graveyard. Two days ago, two orphans had died. I saw their mutilated body parts littering the ground, chewed up by jackals.

The stench of the bodies was unbearable, so we ran across the graveyard as quickly as we could. We passed the small house, the big house, and Father Francis's house. We went up a hill and down again. In the distance I could spot the sea, with the lights of a few fishing boats bobbing up and down. There were small, one-story houses all about us, and endless lines of trees—probably orchards belonging to the villagers.

The team walked on in complete silence. It had been an hour since we had left the orphanage. We had never come this far before. After another few hills, Yusuf finally came to a halt. "See that fruit?" he said. "Those are carobs. First, go up into the trees and have your fill. Then, fill up your bags!"

We had seen this fruit during our deportation, but we had never thought it was edible. The carobs looked like black horns, hanging limply from the branches.

Overcoming my inhibitions, I obeyed Yusuf, picked one of the carobs, and tentatively bit a small piece off. It was really delicious! It was as sweet as jam. I devoured a few of them, spitting out the seeds. I then climbed onto a branch and, straddling it, began filling bags. I quickly filled up two of them. I paused to rest, but the temptation was too much—I began eating again.

The moon was right behind the peak of a mountain, not too far from the horizon. Yusuf began jumping from branch to branch, rushing us along: "Quick! Fill up the bags and let's get out of here!"

I had filled three bags, and the others had done just as many. Our supply would surely last even more than the usual two weeks.

"Thank God!" I whispered to myself. "We've found the cornucopia!"

I was about to jump down when I heard the sound of running feet coming in our direction. I froze. Was it just a random passerby? The sound came closer and closer. Up in the branches, I squinted to see through the leaves.

Some men skidded to a halt right beneath the tree. They saw us in the branches. There were three of them—all young, with long mustaches and beards. My heart was in my throat.

They signaled to us to come down. The two full bags I had placed beside me fell with a thud onto the ground. I tried to carry the third down with me. As I scampered down, one of the men grabbed me and deposited me on the ground. I was terrified.

Yusuf, Nishan, Kevork, and I stood before these swarthy, healthy men. We were full of shame and scared out of our wits. Would they beat us? Kill us? We were like four condemned men facing our three judges, awaiting our verdict. I hoped they would take pity on us, considering our age and our miserable circumstances.

They emptied our measly bags into three large sacks. Then they ordered us, in a language we didn't understand, to climb back up the tree and pick the rest of the carobs. We continued working until their sacks were full. At that point, just as the sun was about to rise, they waved at us and walked away. They seemed to be nervously eyeing the horizon, which was now pink with the sun's first rays.

We stood under the tree, in shock, exchanging terrified glances.

"Thank God that's all they did!" said Yusuf.

"They could have killed us," added Nishan.

"It's almost dawn. Get back up the trees and fill your pockets with any carobs you find. That's all we have time for!" ordered Yusuf.

We jumped into the branches and began picking carobs at a feverish pace. We weren't sure we'd make it back to the orphanage in time, but we had to try our best. As we walked back, I followed my friends with a troubled mind. It was a deserted area, and if they had murdered us, nobody would have been the wiser. I thanked God for watching over my friends and me.

The moon set behind the mountains. We kept up a hectic pace, wading through thick thorny vegetation, cutting our shins and our feet with every step. Suddenly, Nishan stumbled against something, and with a muffled cry of pain he stopped. His toes were covered in blood. Yusuf plucked a couple of leaves from the bush behind him, spat on them, and tied them around Nishan's battered foot. He figured out that Nishan had tripped over the skull of either an ox or a cow.

"Don't cry," he said to Nishan. "This skull belongs to you now. You can smash it into the powder and eat it!"

Nishan took the skull and limped after the rest of us. We were exhausted from walking, but we had to go on. I trudged on, wondering when we would be free of this terrible life, of hunger and thirst, of terror and fear, of trauma and pain.

As we climbed over the hill, we saw Father Francis's home through the leaves of the trees. Back in familiar territory, we hurried down the slope heading toward the graveyard, startling a jackal that fled from us in the underbrush, whining as it ran.

We climbed over the wall behind the gymnasium and emptied our pockets. Yusuf hid the carobs and a few bones under large rocks, concealing it all with twigs and leaves.

We snuck into our dormitories and crawled into bed. Just as we did so, the morning bell rang. I tried my best not to look too tired and to go about my day as if nothing extraordinary had happened during the night.

During the afternoon, while we were all out in the courtyard, Yusuf gathered our team together. "Whatever we brought last night, we'll share with our other friends. Are you all in agreement with this plan?"

We approved unanimously. The leaders of the raiding teams had decided that from now on the bounty of each raid would be shared among all the teams. We would share resources and blunt competition among ourselves.

By that point there were more than forty of these teams active in Antoura, each consisting of four to six boys, and each with a leader who received the blind obedience of those under his command. These leaders were the liaison among the teams, but the other members didn't even know the boys in the other teams. Secrecy was absolutely essential. We were all between the ages of seven and twelve, yet we functioned like an army, keeping everything to ourselves. One loose tongue could undermine our operation. There was an agreement that if a team was caught, its members would take their punishment without ever implicating or denouncing others.

We never discovered who had established this system of raiding parties and the rules that governed their activities. He must have been a rather unconventional boy.

Once in a while, a boy would be expelled from a team for having let something slip, but even then, he was not excluded from enjoying the bounty of the raids—he still received a small percentage of the booty.

If not for the bravery and daring of the boys in these teams, the number of boys who died in the orphanage might have doubled. Many of these boys were true adventurers. I was a timid person, easily perturbed and easily frightened, and the thought of theft seemed absolutely repulsive to me. But the instinct of survival led me into their ranks. Since Krikor's escape, I had no other choice but to become a bold thief.

We weren't doing this because we enjoyed it. We had been pushed into a corner by the administration, and we were being starved to death. Even at that early age, I understood that God would forgive our sins.

‿

A few weeks later, Yusuf led us on another raid, heading in a completely new direction. As we went down a hill, I saw small clearings in the woods, occupied by the ruins of what used to be respectable homes surrounded by gardens or fields. They were all abandoned now; the orchards around the homes had been left untended.

There was no time to count, but I think there were at least two dozen trees in the first orchard we entered—apple, pear, plum, and fig trees. The fruits were small and sweet, and as we filled our pockets and bags, we filled our stomachs, too.

"What luck! No barking dogs, and no thieves to steal from us," commented Nishan.

As the moon slowly went down behind the nearby mountain and the eastern horizon brightened with the early rays of the sun, we walked back to the orphanage without much fear. It was a quiet, breezy night, which was particularly enjoyable on a full stomach. Our route seemed to be very safe; we never got near the houses, which meant that we were too far away even for the dogs to smell us.

The return trip was easy. We were going down a gentle slope. At some point, we startled an animal in the bushes, which bolted across our way and into the woods. It was another one of the hungry jackals that wandered the area, waiting for an orphan to die so it could desecrate his body.

The next day, as usual, each of us found a dark corner and ate our fruit with relish. Though I guarded my food jealously, and I did my best to eat secretly, the other boys could often see my jaws moving, and they realized I had food that they didn't. Sometimes I felt like a villain, so I gave one of my friends an entire plum or a carob.

One morning, Yusuf gathered us together, and after making sure we weren't being overheard, he told us that some other teams were trading their fruit for bread.

What a scandal! They barely gave us any bread at the orphanage. Why sacrifice that sustenance for a few pieces of fruit? Besides, a black market created real danger for all of us. There would be envy, jealousy, and theft among the boys. It would lead to denunciations, arguments, and enmity. Yusuf agreed to speak with the other leaders about the problem.

During class, as Mullah Nejmeddin's voice droned on, I kept thinking of those unfortunate boys who were sacrificing their daily bread for a few figs or a small apple. At our eleven o'clock meal, while nibbling my bread and forcing myself to spoon some cold, tasteless soup into my mouth, I kept noticing how some boys were not eating their bread, instead stuffing the buns into their pockets.

Later, in the courtyard, I observed some of those same boys. One of them walked around with a handful of grapes in his hand. Another was eating plums greedily in a dark corner.

That evening, Yusuf reported to us that the team leaders were putting an end to the trade of fruit and bread. They had also decided that from now on, each team leader would give away some of his team's supplies to the other orphans in his class or his dormitory. Everybody would have a small serving of fruit every day, without having to sacrifice his bread.

The leaders added to their own responsibility. Now they had to feed dozens of additional boys. The raiding teams had to be more active than ever to steal more fruit and vegetables.

Yusuf and the other leaders created a schedule. Each night, only four or five teams left the orphanage—this minimized the chances of getting caught and ensured that different teams did not compete over the same turf. The leaders also organized the hideouts and the routes of each team, allowing for the proper storage and distribution of the stolen food.

The members of the raiding teams, including me, were becoming virtual professionals. We learned how to distinguish the other teams from guards and locals. We quickly climbed up trees and picked the fruit. We even saw better in the dark.

We no longer collected bones. We weren't that desperate anymore. As we expanded the targets of our raids, we found more vegetables, more fruit, more nuts. Fortunately, we lived in a country where fresh produce could be found nine months out of the year.

We had almost forgotten those terrible days when we ate leaves off the trees or flies in the classrooms. We now had plums, peaches, apples, pears, apricots, figs, and grapes, and we had discovered carobs, which, though tough and difficult to chew, were sweet as honey.

Because of the area's famine, most of the locals had locked up their houses and left for the cities, where they thought they had a better chance of finding bread. They had left their gardens and their orchards untended, which was a blessing for us. Our raiding teams were bringing back up to ten full bags of produce. After hiding loot in pre-designated spots, we went to bed in high spirits, knowing that other boys had silently prayed for us under the sheets.

A few orphans in Antoura never asked for any of the goods we brought back from our adventures. They were either küçük beys, the informers and denouncers of other orphans, or they had certain jobs that afforded them extra food, such as working in the kitchen, mess hall, and clinic. These boys considered themselves superior to the other orphans, and they never entertained the idea of tying their fate with ours.

The availability of fruit and vegetables made a huge difference in our lives. The threat of famine greatly decreased, and there was an increased sense of camaraderie as well as a growing willingness to challenge the administration. Despite the threat of punishment and the constant presence of informers, the boys boldly began speaking Armenian among themselves. I even witnessed some of them publicly crossing themselves before meals and before going to sleep.

It had been three years since we had been moved to the orphanage, and, clearly, the administration's attempt to Turkify us was a miserable failure. When we challenged the teachers or the headmaster, we never felt alone. We were one united front, struggling together. If someone did betray us, we cut them off from the fruit and vegetables—quite a punishment, indeed.

‿

In Antoura, we fought a battle against an enemy intent on destroying our identities. We didn't have mothers or fathers, or even good teachers and educators, to guide us and impart their wisdom. The older boys were our role models. We took our cues from them, realizing that they did their best to be good examples. They encouraged us to keep our language alive, pray to our God, and never forget that we were Armenians.

We were always on the lookout for informers, which meant that we lacked trust among ourselves. The administration had succeeded in that arena; they had sown these seeds of distrust. But could we really blame the informers? They were weak-minded, to be sure, but they were hungry, and they were willing to do anything for an extra piece of bread.

But the administration must have realized the longer the battle went on, the more it lost to a bunch of Armenian children.

Did our teachers ever realize that *they* were the ones who strengthened our resolve against them? How could we strive to be like our teachers when they were brutal, sadistic fiends? How could we accept our new Turkish identities when the Turks tasked with our care mercilessly insulted and beat us at the slightest provocation?

All around me were the children and grandchildren of the Armenians who had gone to their graves in the pitiless desert of Syria. We had been spared only because we were still impressionable children. Yet the rebellious streak in us had not been squashed. Even after all the insults, the mistreatment, and the beatings, we continued to wage our desperate struggle.

CHAPTER 7

THE CAVES

IT HAD BEEN SIX MONTHS since the team leaders agreed to distribute their bounty to all the orphans, and the raiding teams were busier than ever. They provided fruit and vegetables to most of the boys once or twice a week.

There had been improvements in the procedures, too: boys stood guard while the teams went out, making sure that no staff members would interfere with the raids.

Despite the secrecy and stealth of these operations, some boys were inevitably caught and punished. Our team's leader, Yusuf, was reported to the staff twice. The first time, the headmaster attempted to extract a confession, but Yusuf claimed complete ignorance about any thefts, categorically denied the charges against him, and insisted that he knew nothing about anyone who belonged to any raiding teams. He spent two days in confinement.

The second time he was caught, he was deprived of food for forty-eight hours. He was released only after receiving a warning in the strongest of terms.

Villagers began visiting the administration to complain that the orphans were robbing them. These men often issued a veiled threat; they stated that they had been merciful, knowing that the thieves were orphans, but they implied that in the future they might use deadly force.

The locals' threats made the administration uncomfortable. After all, the Turks had come to Lebanon, taken over the monastery in Antoura, and transformed it into an orphanage. The locals considered the Turks invaders. The orphanage guards, who were soldiers, were venal and corrupt, and they treated the villagers with disrespect. They often bought things in town without paying for them. In fact, the village grocer assaulted a guard who failed to pay for a tin of tobacco.

"At least we steal because we're hungry," said Murad. "The guards have full stomachs, yet they still steal, just for enjoyment."

"We're Armenians, and it's wrong for us to steal," philosophized Kevork. "They're Turks; theft is part of their character. Wherever they go, Turks always become thieves."

"Be ready for tonight!" interrupted Yusuf, in his usual curt manner. "We'll be going for God knows how long."

"What do you mean? Where are we going?" asked Nishan.

"Don't worry about it. Just do what I say," said Yusuf before walking away.

I suddenly realized that Yusuf was talking about running away from the orphanage.

೨

By that point, the administration had increased its security precautions. There were thirty orphanage guards, and they watched the storerooms twenty-four hours a day, stationed themselves in the vegetable garden at night, and constantly patrolled the perimeter of the wall.

More and more, the boys talked about escape. We were of two minds. On one hand, the orphanage was a purgatory, full of beatings and insults. On the other hand, it was a safe haven, an institution that we knew— though hungry, we were guaranteed at least *some* food. If we escaped, we would be spending weeks and possibly months in the forests and the mountains, without the little food we received in the orphanage, with no guarantee of safety, and without even a bed to sleep in.

"What do you think? Should we go with Yusuf?" asked Nishan.

"Yusuf knows what he's doing. Even if we die out there, it'd be better than dying in here," replied Murad.

"If we die here we'll become food for the jackals. Up in the mountains, at least our bodies will feed the foxes," joked Kevork.

"A few days ago four boys escaped. Nobody's been looking for them, nobody's even been talking about them," added Murad.

"Let's run away and face whatever may come," concluded Kevork, grinning wistfully. Our team dispersed in the courtyard, each of us struggling with our thoughts.

I wondered about the boys who had already escaped. Were they still hiding up in the mountains, or had they reached the cities? Was there enough food in the cities? Was famine not a threat there? I had no answers, just questions.

Yusuf appeared as soon as darkness fell.

"Boys, let's get the hell out of this place!" he said. "There's nothing left for us to do here. Say a prayer and follow me!" He led us to the back of the gymnasium. None of us carried anything; we had no earthly possessions to slow us down.

We climbed over the fence and ran toward the graveyard. I could hardly believe it. We were free! I was free!

I looked back through the thick darkness and traced the outline of the orphanage, that hellish edifice where I had spent three entire years—three years full of suffering, hunger, pain, and fear. I was now eight years old. I had shed my indecisiveness and grown much more confident. I followed Yusuf and my other friends with a steady, deliberate gait.

We passed the graveyard. I crossed myself automatically, thinking of the hundreds who were buried under our feet. I prayed that God would watch over the boys we were leaving behind in the orphanage, and that there would be no more bodies buried here and mutilated by jackals.

As we passed the "small house" and "big house," I hoped that the people who lived there would forgive us of our sins, which had been committed only to survive. As we approached Father Francis's home, we heard the mad barking of his dog, which had so often terrorized us during our nocturnal adventures.

We kept going, following in Yusuf's steps. We had never come this way before. We climbed over hills, down into valleys, and through thick, thorny undergrowth. Yusuf came to a halt at the bottom of a slope. We could hear the sound of gurgling water coming from nearby. On the flanks of the mountains around us we could see the occasional glimmering light, indicating the presence of homes.

It was early spring. The fragrances of thousands of flowers and trees hung in the night air. We paused to catch our breath. "I know you can't see right now, but there is a river down in the valley, and on both banks is a thick forest. There are green trees and beautiful flowers everywhere. I promise you, boys, you'll love what you'll see in the morning," said Yusuf.

"Where are we going to hide? There may be passersby," asked Nishan anxiously.

"Don't worry. There are caves in the forest," replied Yusuf.

"There'll be jackals and foxes there. Will we live with them?" asked Kevork naively.

"Once they see us, they won't dare come close. They'll be scared of us," assured Yusuf.

We walked some more, finally reaching the entrance of a cave. This was no luxury accommodation. A huge tear in the rock face opened into a deep, low cavern full of animal waste. The stench was terrible, and as we walked in, we couldn't avoid stepping on dried dung.

Exhausted from walking all night, we lay down, each trying our best to find a dry piece of ground. Within minutes we were all asleep.

When we woke up, the sun was already high in the sky. We could now see our cave. It was deep and humid, and in the warmth of the day, the animal waste was even more malodorous.

Yusuf was missing. We didn't know what to do. Where could he have gone without telling us? None of us dared leave the cave to look for him; we might not find our way back, or we might be spotted outside by a local. We were also very hungry. Even though we were accustomed to not eating till eleven, we used to have classes and brutal teachers to take our minds off our hunger. Now, sitting idly in the cave, we could think of nothing other than food and Yusuf.

We didn't speak much—we had become accustomed to communicating with glances and silent gestures. Where was Yusuf? Then we heard some twigs breaking outside. Yusuf entered the cave, carrying two large bundles of branches and twigs. His pockets were full of fruit. He dropped his load and said: "Eat up, and afterward help me collect branches. These won't be enough, we need to gather more. We need to camouflage the entrance of the cave, boys."

"Where did you find the fruit?" asked Kevork.

"They're easy to find in the forest. Eat up, this is today's lunch," replied Yusuf. He sat down and grabbed a piece.

We didn't know the names of these wild fruits, but they were all fresh and juicy. Some were bitter, but still very delicious. At first I hesitated to eat one of the stranger fruits, but Kevork nudged me. "Don't think too much about it, we've eaten much worse!" he joked.

"From now on, we'll mostly live on fruit and roots," said Yusuf. "We won't have any more bread. The bread is back at the orphanage. Our friends will have our share." He divided the remaining fruit into two piles. "This pile will be for lunch, and that one for dinner," he stated. "Don't ask about tomorrow. God will provide."

Nishan asked for our attention. "Starting today, we must say grace before every meal," he said. "At the orphanage, we would be punished for doing this, but now we're free. We'll no longer cross ourselves hiding under our sheets at nights—we'll pray out loud, proudly, and in Armenian!"

Yusuf had us pledge that we would never speak Turkish again. He asked us to correct him whenever he slipped into Turkish, which he often did.

The cave, then, became our Armenian school, our Armenian church, our bastion of our Armenian identities.

But as we spent the day cloistered inside the cave, I realized it was also a self-imposed prison. We couldn't risk being spotted outside. At least in the orphanage there were *some* adults who could protect us. Now we were utterly alone.

Yusuf rose, went to the entrance of the cave, and looked out through the branches and leaves. Across the valley he could see several villages, and he could even distinguish men working in the fields. "We can't stay here too long," he said. "We've got to find someplace else to hide."

"Where are we going to go?" asked Nishan. "Wouldn't it be better to go back to the orphanage?"

"That's not an option. We just have to find a safer hideout," declared Yusuf. He seemed anxious, and that unsettled us. We were accustomed to seeing him resolute and decisive.

"Sit down and relax, Yusuf, let's think about what to do now," said Murad.

"I think we should go back to the orphanage, too," interjected Kevork, speaking uneasily. "Whatever happens, we'll be with our friends, and even if we die we'll die with them."

"Do you know how many teams escaped the orphanage last night, just like we did?" snapped back Yusuf. "Returning is not an option. Even if it was a mistake to escape, we'd be making yet another mistake if we go back."

It had been less than twenty-four hours since our escape, and there was already dissension in our ranks. We still weren't sure what was better—to tolerate the conditions at the orphanage and have some assurance of survival, or to be free and face an uncertain future. We discussed the issue for hours.

As the sun sank toward the western horizon, Yusuf distributed a handful of fruit to each of us. There wouldn't be any bread for as long as we stayed in the mountains and woods. "Don't worry, you'll get used to it," he said, realizing our disappointed expressions. "You'll soon realize that fruits and vegetables are enough for us to survive."

"Don't worry, we're already used to it," smiled Kevork. "If we had relied on those tiny buns of bread we would have been dead long ago."

"In a week or two most of the fruit will have ripened—plums, peaches, apricots, grapes. So just be patient, and soon we'll be getting fat," said Yusuf, trying to lighten the mood.

"Enough about your fruit! First, find us a decent place to sleep," exclaimed Nishan. "Once we have a roof over our head, we'll start worrying about the variety in our diet."

"Nishan is right," agreed Kevork. "You said this cave won't do. Where will we go? Where will we sleep tonight?"

"Just give me some time. Today and tomorrow I'll comb through the area and find us a better cave," promised Yusuf. He was perturbed by the rebellious attitude of the boys under his command.

When darkness fell, it was finally safe for us to go outside. We breathed the clean, crisp air, stretched our arms and legs, and sat down near the mouth of our cave, with our backs against the trees.

It was a cool, breezy night. We heard the gurgling of the stream from below in the valley. Across the bank, we saw isolated lights in the villages on the mountains. In the distance, we heard the growling of dogs, and we hoped they were not attacking other teams that had escaped the orphanage. Despite the calmness of the night, every time a bird flitted from branch to branch above us in the trees, we jumped up with a startle, thinking that we had been discovered.

A few hours later, Yusuf wished us a good night and left to explore the area, trying to find a better cave. He had a wonderful sense of direction. Even though he had never been this far from the orphanage before, he instinctively knew which way to go, and he always found his way back. He also could distinguish edible wild fruits from inedible ones, and he even knew which ones tasted good and which didn't. When did he learn all this?

Another reason we trusted Yusuf was the large knife he carried in the pocket of his uniform. This knife had dozens of uses. When picking fruit or stealing vegetables, it came in handy as a digger. More important, it was our only means of self-defense if we ever faced danger. Yusuf didn't allow any of us to ever handle the knife. In our minds, it took on legendary characteristics. We truly believed that the knife would protect us from any danger, without even wondering whether Yusuf knew how to use it as a weapon.

Later that night, we heard footsteps stop at the entrance, and Yusuf entered after pulling away the improvised door of branches and leaves. Before saying anything, he emptied his pockets. He had collected more fruit, though most of it was not quite ripe enough.

"Eat as much as you can," he commanded. "We'll leave later tonight. I found us another cave. It's not as big, but it's safer and more comfortable. We'll stay there, but we'll still be on the lookout for better shelter. We can stay in the woods until it starts getting cold, and when we can't take the cold anymore, we'll decide what to do. We'll either go back to the orphanage, or ... We'll figure it out."

Yusuf looked exhausted and almost distraught. He was only thirteen or fourteen years old, yet he was shouldering the responsibility of keeping four younger boys alive and healthy. None of us argued with him. We would stay in the woods until winter.

The next evening, as the sun disappeared behind the mountains and the shadows lengthened all around us, we filled our bags with fruit and stepped out of the cave that had been our abode for barely forty-eight hours. We followed Yusuf in a tight column, taking a winding, curvy, overgrown path through the woods. It was lined with countless wild carob trees. Most of the fruit was not ripe enough to be edible, but it improved our mood to know that within weeks we'd have a huge supply of fruit.

The valley narrowed, and the path was barely discernible. We heard the shuffling of paws in the bushes and occasionally saw the glistening eyes of jackals, but they didn't bother us, and we kept marching forward. It seemed that humans had not walked this path for many centuries.

Yusuf abruptly came to a halt. In front of us was a large cave with a half-concealed opening. Inside, the cavern was about the size of a large room. We set up our supplies in one corner and tried our best to find the most comfortable spot to sleep.

We woke up late the next morning, a freedom we never had at the orphanage. We looked out of the cave with awe and wonder—beneath us were thick forests, and around us peaks of divine mountains. It was a beautiful place to call home, even if we were living like animals.

We couldn't see any homes or villages in the mountains, which meant that we couldn't be seen, either. Still, Yusuf was adamant about covering the entrance with branches and leaves so we'd be safe from prying eyes. We could still hear the stream down in the valley, so we didn't have to worry about finding potable water. As for food, the forest would have to provide.

In the afternoon heat, as we sat in a circle in the cave and munched on fruit, we discussed the night's plans. "This cave is much safer than the other one," announced Yusuf. "I don't think we run the risk of being seen by anybody here."

Our quiet cheer was torn apart by the sound of a rifle shot. The echoes of the shot reverberated across the valley and the mountains. It wasn't particularly close to the cave, but it terrified us. We exchanged nervous glances, trying to find some comfort in each other's gazes. It had only been a few hours since our arrival in the cave, and already our illusions of safety had shattered.

We spent the entire day inside the cave, making sure our improvised door completely covered the entrance. As night fell, we waited to hear Yusuf's orders.

"Come on, boys, cross yourselves and follow me!" ordered Yusuf, jumping to his feet. We left the cave and began walking through a thicket. We journeyed for a while, sometimes climbing up, sometimes going down. Suddenly, Yusuf stopped, went down to his knees, and put his ear against the ground. We had no idea what he was doing. Eventually he stood back up, and since we weren't allowed to speak while marching, he signaled us to follow him and continued on.

From the peak of a hill, we saw no homes and no fields. Across the valley, on the flank of the opposite mountain, we spotted a few lights, winking weakly in the opaque night, reminding us that we were still on Earth, among human beings.

Yusuf kept walking. We couldn't ask him questions, and we had no idea where he was headed. Probably for the first time, I began doubting him, and a strange fear took hold of my heart. I almost panicked. Kevork was right in front of me, and though I couldn't say anything to him, I nudged him and tried to communicate my fears with hand signals and muted movements of the lips.

He signaled me to be quiet, but, eventually, when we paused for a few seconds, he turned around and whispered: "Are you afraid? Do you regret having escaped the orphanage? Don't! Don't you worry! God will take care of us, and whatever may come, our fate is in his hands."

We kept walking. As the horizon grew purple with the rising sun, we looked across the valley and toward the distant sea, where we saw small, isolated villages in the forest, waking up with the new day.

Yusuf pointed to a few carob trees nearby. We climbed into the branches and filled our bags, as well as our stomachs, with the juicy fruits. This tiny bounty made the entire march worthwhile.

We rushed back toward our cave. Winding our way across the mountains, we spied villagers going to their fields in the valley. Some were mounted on donkeys, along with large sacks of grains and fruit that they were probably taking to the nearest town to sell or barter.

Finally, we arrived home. We dropped our bags in the corner and lay down on the hard rock, exhausted. For three years our lives had been a constant struggle against famine, and even though we were free now, we still could not rid ourselves of the specter of hunger. Free or not, we still had to struggle for every morsel.

Outside, the sun rose high in the sky, inundating the valley and the mountains with light and warmth. In the cave, we sat in a circle, snacking on carobs and commenting on the night's events.

Yusuf admitted that we had been lost and had wandered about aimlessly. "If we hadn't found the carobs at the very end of our expedition, we would've returned empty-handed," he confessed.

"There's no need to fret," assured Murad. "What we found is better than nothing. It'll last us a couple of days. Think of our friends back in the orphanage. God knows how many of them have died since we left, or how many are in the clinic because of malnutrition."

We had become brothers, bonding in the worst of times, suffering from hunger and disease, constantly facing death. Our friendships could survive any challenge, and they had become even stronger now that we shared the cave. But without Yusuf, we would have been lost. We depended on him for guidance, leadership, moral support, and most important, food. We relied on him to survive. He was the epitome of a great leader, who was willing to sacrifice everything for his squad.

As the days passed, we established a certain routine. During the daytime, we spent most of our time in the cave, chatting and reminiscing. We recalled the orphanage, the friends we had left behind, the falakha and the sadistic teachers, the constant hunger. We also shared accounts of our hometowns, of our families and our friends in better times. Whenever we ate, we always made sure to record how much food remained at our disposal; our guideline was to always have two or three days' supplies stored in the cave.

When evening descended, Yusuf would stand up, proceed to the cavern entrance, check the surroundings, and calmly inform us: "Boys, night is falling. Get ready."

Late one night, we left our cave and walked toward an area that we didn't know very well. In the dark, we stumbled about and tripped on rocks. There was no proper footpath. We simply dropped into the valley and climbed over a few hillocks. Soon we heard the distant barking of a dog. That meant homes were nearby, or perhaps an entire village—which meant fields, gardens, and orchards.

Yusuf guided us closer, and we noticed several carob trees ahead. We picked a bunch and devoured them almost without chewing. They were drier than the ones we'd had before, more pleasant to the palate.

"Eat up, boys!" whispered Yusuf, relishing his success.

For the past two weeks we'd been surviving exclusively on a diet of fruit, mostly carobs. But we didn't complain. In fact, we hadn't noticed any difference in our general level of health. If anything, we were in higher spirits. Nature was kind to us. Even when we didn't find proper fields or orchards, we could always count on the wild carob trees, which provided us with plenty of nutrition. We were like birds, satisfying ourselves with the bounty of nature and asking for nothing more.

But tonight, it seemed, Yusuf planned for more than the usual carobs. Instead of retracing our steps to the cave, he led us forward. Within a few minutes, we reached a small orchard, and all around us were branches overburdened with pears and plums. We were overjoyed. Some of us emptied our bags of carobs to make room for the more delectable fruit.

"You like what you see?" smugly asked Yusuf. He said that we could live for many months by just raiding this garden. "Boys, you can forget about that orphanage now," he added. "It's nothing but a memory."

Ironically, Yusuf's words reminded me of the boys we had left behind. Were they still alive? Were they still there? Was the war still raging? Were they still massacring Armenians? Was our absence the topic of discussion among our old friends?

"Wait for me here, I'll be right back," said Yusuf, and he left without another word.

We exchanged anxious glances. We didn't dare take a single step without Yusuf's guidance. If we were caught by villagers, we wouldn't even be capable of resisting. We didn't know the way back. Without his leadership, we would probably surrender and go back to the orphanage, or die in the wilderness.

Yusuf returned with pockets full of more plums, some apricots, and even some edible herbs. "Eat up!" he said. "Don't be afraid. I don't know what these herbs are called, but I know we can eat them, and they taste all right."

"Why did you leave us alone? Why didn't you take us with you?" admonished Murad.

"Someone might have spotted the whole team. By myself, I can sneak into the gardens undetected," Yusuf explained. "Besides, there could come a day when I'm not with you. You should be able to take care of yourselves."

"Then why did you bring us all the way here if you were going to go at it alone?" complained Nishan.

"Don't fret. I'm not going anywhere. I'll be with you until the end. But accidents happen, and we can't foresee the future," answered Yusuf, trying to calm us all down.

"I think it'd be better for us to go back to the orphanage," mumbled Kevork. We all somewhat agreed. At least in the orphanage we shared our misery with our friends.

"I promise, boys, I won't leave you," Yusuf assured us. "Whether inside the orphanage, or out here, we'll always stick together. Now let's go back to the cave, and be ready to raid again tonight."

For our next nighttime excursion, we again descended into the valley, following Yusuf's footsteps. As the moon rose into the sky, it cast a pale glow that guided our steps. On this night, at least, we wouldn't be walking blindly.

Soon we found a narrow footpath lined by pear and plum trees. Their fruit was still unripe, and Yusuf didn't allow us to pick them. He had better targets in mind. We reached a fence surrounding a decent-sized garden. All was still. There wasn't even the slightest breeze to ruffle the leaves on the trees.

We climbed over the fence, and following Yusuf's lead, each of us climbed up a tree. They were all plum trees, their fruit almost ripe. As usual, we first devoured as many as we could, relishing their sweet taste. Then we filled our bags and pockets with as many plums as we could fit.

When we climbed down, we euphorically showed each other our huge, juicy plums and then returned to our cave. We emptied our pockets and placed the full bags of fruit against the wall. It was almost dawn, and from the hamlets in the valley we could hear the crowing of roosters and the barking of dogs.

"How long will all this fruit last us?" asked Murad.

"It depends on our appetite, of course, but I think we should be fine for five or six days," replied Yusuf.

"So we'll be prisoners of this cave for the next week or so," sighed Kevork as he lay down on the hard floor.

"I think we should all get some sleep, we're all tired," said Yusuf. He lay down as well.

I tried to follow their lead, but despite my exhaustion, I couldn't sleep. As usual, I reminisced. I remembered home, my family, the orphanage at Hama, the friends I had left behind, the stench of the rotting bodies in the graveyard. Eventually, I drifted into sleep; when I awoke, the others were sitting around me, rubbing their eyes and yawning.

"Are you hungry? You couldn't get any sleep?" Nishan asked Kevork.

"Both," replied Kevork.

"Well, eat and then go back to sleep. It's not like we have anything else to do all day," said Murad. Yusuf was still snoring in his corner.

But instead of sleeping, we sat up, discussing our next adventure.

"Who knows what it'll be? Yusuf will always be the one who decides," said Nishan.

"Why are you worried about it? We have enough food to last us another week. Don't think too much of the future. God will provide," said Murad.

"I disagree," said Kevork. "We should try to make plans as early as possible."

⌣

Once, an old man from a nearby village brought us bread. He placed the bread at the entrance of the cave and left without a word, without even informing us of his kindness.

We were shocked. There were still kind people in the world? We knew hunger was ravaging the countryside, and yet this man had decided to share what little he had with a bunch of half-feral orphans living in a cave. We brought the bread inside and sat around it in a circle. It had been months since we had tasted bread. We devoured it quickly.

"That was good, but a bit difficult to swallow," said Murad. "Was it wheat bread?"

"We've just eaten bread, and you're wondering what it's made of?" mocked Kevork. "For all I care, it could be made of barley, or whatever, as long as it's bread."

"The bread at the orphanage was better," said Nishan.

"The bread at the orphanage was bread only in name," retorted Kevork.

"May God bless that old man," I muttered.

"I'm worried, though. What if that old man tells people about us? What if they come looking for us?" said Yusuf.

"Don't you think they have better things to do than look for us?" replied Murad.

The cave was safe from passersby and from the nearby villages, but now we knew for sure that one person, at least, knew exactly where we were. Thankfully, nothing came of it, and nobody bothered us.

The days passed monotonously—they were long and warm, while the nights were short and crisp. However, our supply of fruit ran low. Yusuf was becoming anxious.

On our next raid, we found a large vineyard. We separated and immediately went to work, alternatively eating the grapes and filling our bags. The grapes weren't quite ripe yet and had a bitter taste to them, but they were good enough.

On our way back toward the cave, as we climbed back over a fence, Nishan's feet slipped and he fell, smashing his face against the ground. He immediately burst into tears. Yusuf jumped toward him and covered Nishan's mouth right away. "Don't cry! Be brave!" he admonished, and he lifted Nishan off the ground. We all gathered around Nishan and did our best to encourage him to keep going forward.

We retraced our steps to the cave, heading uphill, while Nishan limped and whimpered. We had to stop a few times to let him rest. He seemed to be seriously injured. In the cave, we gathered around Nishan to examine him more closely. There were several open wounds on his shins, and the skin on his foot had peeled off. He was bleeding profusely.

Yusuf found a few leaves that were mixed in with the grapes, and he gave them to Nishan. "Go outside and urinate on these!" he commanded.

Nishan glared at Yusuf in complete surprise. We, too, were shocked. But seeing that our leader was being earnest, Nishan went outside and did what he was told.

Yusuf used one of the soiled leaves to clean Nishan's blood and used the others to cover the wounds. For bandages, he used some ripped strips of the bags that we used to steal fruit. Yusuf's stature grew even larger in our eyes: not only was he a good leader and an expert thief, he was even a nurse!

We needed to get some sleep before noon, when we would have a meal and enjoy more grapes. Now that it was the season, we knew the grapes would get only more delicious with the passage of the weeks.

Nishan and Kevork both immediately fell asleep, back-to-back. We could already hear their steady breathing. Nishan occasionally spoke in his sleep. "He's dreaming," said Yusuf. "It sounds like he's fighting with someone."

A few minutes later, Nishan woke up with a start, swiveling around as if he was looking for someone. "Where is he?" he asked.

"Who are you talking about?" asked Yusuf.

"My brother. I was back at home. I was wrestling with him . . ."

Similar scenes had occurred every night at the orphanage. Boys had dreamed that they were back home, woken up, and remained for a few minutes in a strange limbo between their dreams and their lives.

Yusuf was the only one who didn't seem to dream of such things. He lived only in the present, with no time for flights of fantasy. At night, he often left alone, mapping the area mentally and finding new targets for our raids. Even in the morning, he often ventured outside, but always returned unscathed and unharmed, and sometimes with pockets full of carobs.

Yusuf also sustained us mentally. He was a great storyteller, and he often entertained us by recounting folktales, peppering the stories with his own embellishments and painting vivid pictures of his characters, whom we loved, whether they were good or evil.

We often fantasized that one day we would be like the heroes of Yusuf's stories—we would have flaming swords, ride swift steeds, storm forts, conquer castles, and litter the ground around us with the bodies of our enemies. Then we would share our spoils equally and live happily ever after.

Life on the lam taught us more than the teachers at the orphanage. We learned the basics of survival, the ethics of self-sacrifice, and the sharing of resources. Moreover, we trusted one another with our very lives. We had created our own little family of boys, without mothers or fathers. The wilderness was our school, and Yusuf our guide. All we had to do was learn from him, and we, too, would know every nook and cranny of the mountains.

Once, a small animal, the likes of which we had never seen, appeared at the entrance of our cave. It looked around before darting down into the valley, where it climbed a tree and began munching on something.

"That's a squirrel," declared Yusuf. "If we could only catch it, I think my knife would be enough to separate the skin from the flesh. We could eat the flesh raw, without cooking, and the fur would keep us warm." He focused his attention on it.

The squirrel cracked a nut, ate the insides, and threw away the hard shell. Its head was on a swivel, constantly turning left and right, and it ate as if someone was about to take the nuts away from it. Yusuf surreptitiously began approaching the animal. But at the last second, it turned its head, noticed Yusuf coming, and darted away into the bushes.

"What a shame! It would've been delicious," lamented Nishan.

That squirrel had the entirety of the mountains, the valley, and the forests as its home. It lived in complete freedom, while we humans couldn't even step outside our cave without fear. As if reminding us of our lack of liberty, a column of smoke rose from across the valley—probably from a fireplace that was warming a home.

If we looked carefully, we could see several children playing in the courtyard of a hovel, deep in the valley. They had a dog that was fetching their sticks. From the entrance of our cave, we burned with envy. Our own childhoods had long since ended.

We watched crows descend into the valley. They must have smelled something.

Yusuf jumped to his feet. Why had the crows flown there? He had to know. And besides, he had missed the squirrel, but now he had a chance of catching a crow. We followed him with our eyes all the way down into the valley. He was swift as a fox, moving like a shadow among the trees.

Until Yusuf returned, we didn't speak a word. When he reappeared, he smiled at our obvious relief. "What? You thought I wouldn't come back?" he chuckled.

He laid two full bags on the floor and sat down, tired and panting. He had brought back some delicious almonds. We immediately attacked the bags, breaking the shells with loose rocks and devouring the delectable nuts.

"Are there a lot of almond trees nearby?" asked Murad.

"Just a few, but they're huge!" replied Yusuf. "They'll never run out of almonds!"

"Is it really a good idea to go to the trees during the daytime? Won't we be seen?"

"It's better to go at night, yes. Don't worry about that now, just eat!"

In fact, we soon we had to completely conceal ourselves during daytime. There were more people than ever before in the valley. It was harvest time, and the villagers were gathering fruit and nuts from the trees there, just as we had done for months.

Yusuf soon decided on a more drastic course of action. "We need to move again," he announced one evening.

We all saw the necessity of finding new shelter, but we were anxious. This cave had sheltered us for months. It had been our first real home after escaping from the orphanage, and now we hoped to find some place just as warm and welcoming.

Kevork and Nishan kept staring at the cave's empty walls, as if committing every twist and bend of the rock to memory. Once again, they had to abandon their home.

"You sit tight and wait here," said Yusuf. "I'll go look for a good cave. Just stay here and eat, you're going to need the energy." He walked into the night.

While Yusuf was gone, we heard the distant barking of dogs, and we were afraid that it was targeted at our leader. We heard villagers in the valley calling to each other; we hoped that they weren't calling after Yusuf. Every shout sounded to us like a bellicose threat.

"Here I am!" announced Yusuf upon his return. "Not only did I find us a new cave, but I even got us a bunch of pears! Eat up!" He emptied his pockets, which were full of the juicy fruit. When he sat down among us, he explained that he found a big cave, with wild fruit trees nearby. He planned our move for the next evening.

I didn't feel particularly cheerful about this move. We'd be in unfamiliar territory, even farther away from the relative safety of the orphanage, and winter was approaching. What would we do when the cold winds blew? My friends, too, were worried. I hung my head in despair, hoping that God would protect us.

"What's wrong with you?" Yusuf asked. "Don't you wonder where we're going, too. Don't be so downcast. Eat your fruit and thank the Lord that we're still alive and healthy!"

He was right, in a sense. We had all the fruit we wanted, and our lives weren't regimented like they had been at the orphanage. We had no fear of beatings. We felt no pressure to become Muslims and Turks. What else could we want? In Yusuf's mind at least, we should have had no complaints.

We spent the night in a limbo of half-sleep. It would be our last night in our cave shelter. The flies and mosquitoes were terribly active that night, and they kept biting me through my uniform, the last vestige of my stay at the Antoura orphanage. In the distance, I heard the hooting of an owl. I kept wondering what the poor bird was lamenting.

Suddenly I felt movement at my feet. I jumped up and saw the glowing eyes of a small predator, about to bite me. I called to Yusuf, who was deep in sleep.

"What's wrong? What do you need?" he asked, rubbing his eyes.

"There's an animal in here!" I answered.

"It wasn't a dream, was it?"

"No! I'm telling you, there's an animal in the cave!"

"It's probably already gone. It must have been a jackal."

"But the jackals stay at the cemetery near the orphanage!"

"They must have smelled us and come here," he shrugged.

I could no longer sleep. I couldn't put the incident out of my mind. The next day, as the others chatted and joked, I still felt the breath of the jackal against the soles of my feet. Morning passed, and we ate our fruit, and I still could think only of that jackal.

When the sun went down, we grabbed our bags of fruit and followed our leader. I cast one final glance at the friendly cave that had sheltered us for months.

I was at the rear of our column. As we marched, my pace was slow, and my mind, instead of reflecting on the future, kept recalling the past. In the past three years, I had been forced to leave home, been deported to the desert, survived at the orphanage in Hama, and suffered at the orphanage in Antoura. Now I wandered the wilderness and subsisted on wild fruit. What was the future? More misery? More deprivation? The life of a wild animal?

As we crossed hills and fields, we descended into the valley. The sound of the stream grew louder. Yusuf didn't bother looking back, and we did our best to keep pace with him. Many times we slipped and stumbled, but we jumped right back to our feet. We could hear the small animals following us through the bushes. It seemed like they were mischievously playing hide-and-seek with us.

Finally, Yusuf came to a halt on some flat ground in front of a cave. This was our new home. The entrance was screened by dozens of trees, which provided some protection.

We went inside. This cave was larger and deeper than our last shelter, but the darkness was absolutely impenetrable, so we couldn't ascertain whether the floor was clean or covered by animal droppings.

We put down the bags of fruit and sat down. It was much colder than our previous home. We could see nothing. "Try to get some sleep," drowsily suggested Yusuf. "We'll arrange everything in the morning."

After a sleepless night, the sun illuminated the inside of the cave. Our spirits rose as we realized that it was a very good hiding place, hidden from view, and far from farms and villages. Yusuf conducted a thorough inspection. He was satisfied: he saw no human footprints or animal tracks.

We sat outside the entrance, under the sunlight, and tried to warm our stiff muscles. We rubbed our hands and our half-frozen feet and toes. Yusuf continued his inspection outside the cave, making sure there were no paths leading to us. The nearby mountains meant that it was highly unlikely that villagers would wander in our direction. Again satisfied with his findings, Yusuf sat down with us under the sun.

"Bring the bags of fruit outside, we'll eat here!" he proclaimed.

We had enough fruit for another couple of days. But Yusuf was compulsive about planning ahead. He called for another excursion into the woods for that night.

We had no idea where to find fruit. We were in alien territory, and we heard the baying of jackals and foxes all night. At least the animals' presence indicated the absence of other humans.

That night, we climbed slopes through thorny bushes and rough terrain. Eventually, we reached a hamlet surrounded by several large vineyards.

Yusuf guided us to the fence of one particularly vast vineyard. We jumped over the fence and immediately dispersed to collect grapes. Unfortunately, the grapes had already been harvested. We found some lone clusters here and there, and we ate what we found, but our bags remained hopelessly empty.

When Yusuf signaled to us, we all retreated to a small grove of fruit trees. Desperately, we inspected the branches for fruit, and we did find a few plums, apricots, and pears, but nothing worth this effort. We filled as much of our bags as we could.

Again we retreated, and behind a nearby hill, we regrouped and inspected our bags. We had to find more before returning to our cave, but we also had to remember that we had deviated from our planned route. We needed to make sure that we didn't get lost in the dark night.

We went around a hill and again found some solitary wild pears and a few bunches of ripened almonds. It was getting hopeless. At this point, there was nothing to do but return to the safety of our cave.

Fortunately, fate smiled on us. On our way back, we came across a grove of trees with large, juicy, ripe carobs, the likes of which we had rarely seen. We devoured as many as we could, and filled the rest of the bags to the brim. We were content now. Our haul would probably last us two weeks.

We could now go back to the cave without distraction, with full stomachs, and in high spirits. There was no path to follow, but Yusuf seemed to know exactly where he was going.

As the roofs of the village homes became visible in the faint light, we headed home. With every step, it got colder. The wind seemed to get trapped in the bowl-shaped valley.

Back at the cave, I reflected on the months since we had escaped the orphanage. I was getting sick of life in the woods. We had spent several months without seeing another human face, without eating a hot meal, without any clothes but our old and tattered uniforms. We would freeze to death once winter set in.

"Brothers, don't you think it would be a good idea to go back home?" I muttered, looking at Yusuf out of the corner of my eye.

"You miss the orphanage?" asked Yusuf.

"It's cold, and it's going to get so much colder. Can we survive in these mountains by ourselves?" I asked, addressing everyone. Nishan and Kevork said nothing, but it was obvious that they agreed with me.

"We'll see," muttered Yusuf.

We were all exhausted from our night's excursion, but it was too cold to sleep. All night, we tossed and turned on the rocky ground. Eventually, the sun peeked over the summit of the mountains. The wind was still chilly, but soon we heard the playful jittering of the birds as they flitted from branch to branch, and the young rays of the sun reached the front of our cave. We gathered in the sunlit spot outside the entrance and lay down, more tired than we had ever been since leaving the orphanage.

The warmth finally lulled us into a numb sleep. When I woke up, the sun was scorching my face, and someone was shaking my arm.

"Get up!" said Yusuf. "You'll get sick lying on the ground all day. You'd better not get sick here in the mountains."

I sat up and looked around me. The sun was already high in the sky. I moved to the shade of a tree, still half asleep, and my mind wandered off in reminiscences.

"It's past noon! Come into the cave and let's have our lunch!" called out Yusuf.

We all filed into our new home, and Yusuf gave us each two carobs, five wild pears, and five wild plums. This was a large meal and difficult to finish. Lunch lasted quite a while. It was peppered with conversations and jokes, and we were back in high spirits.

But that evening, menacing clouds formed in the horizon. As darkness descended, the cool breeze turned into a bitingly cold gale, and it began raining torrentially. Droplets of water soon dripped down from the ceiling of our cave.

We passed an extremely uncomfortable night. In the morning, the rain kept battering the earth, and it was impossible to leave the cave. Aside from Yusuf and Murad, we were practically frozen stiff, our teeth chattering uncontrollably.

"The cold came quickly," complained Kevork.

"Won't we see the sun again this year?" joked Nishan.

"Don't worry, the sun will come back to the sky," encouraged Yusuf. "Don't worry, it'll get warmer, it's not winter yet. Besides, boys, soon we'll go . . ."

"Where? Where will we go?" interjected Nishan, but Yusuf's cryptic statement remained unanswered for a few seconds, hanging in midair. I thought of the orphanage. I wanted to be in a warm bed, regardless of the cost.

"Don't worry," continued Yusuf. "Two more weeks in the mountains, and we'll go back to the orphanage."

These words were like music to my ears.

It is strange that these mountains and forests, which had been so welcoming, which had provided us every necessity, were now becoming our enemies. We actually missed the orphanage where we were beaten and abused.

The next day dawned sunny and warm. The dripping branches and twigs seemed to be extending toward the sunlight, and the birds and squirrels were scrambling about again. As we walked out of the cave, we had never appreciated the sun so much.

During lunch, Yusuf announced that later that night we would go on one more excursion to gather food. He reckoned that it would be our last nocturnal adventure.

As soon as night fell, we left the shelter of the cave and began going up the slope, using the same improvised path of our previous excursion. The way was muddy, and water had pooled in ditches. Yusuf bounded from rock to rock, like a wild sheep, advancing without ever looking back. Murad fell flat on his face in the mud, and his entire uniform, already old and thin, was now covered in slick mud. The rest of us advanced carefully, doing our best to follow in Yusuf's exact tracks, ignoring the scratching of the thorny bushes.

It was very cold, and our limbs were shaking no matter how hard we tried to hold them steady. We eventually found a few wild pears and plums still hanging desperately to half-frozen branches. We didn't bother eating;

we just filled our bags and pockets as quickly as possible. On the return trip, we deviated slightly from our path and went by the carob trees, picking as many of them as would fit in our bags and pockets.

The cold air blasted us as soon as we walked through the cave entrance. The situation was becoming untenable. Calmly but decisively, Yusuf said: "This is the last fruit we'll have to live on. Whether we finish it in three days or five days, I don't know. But once we're out of fruit, we'll be going straight back to the orphanage."

Our faces immediately brightened up. The gleam returned to our eyes. We missed our friends, the classrooms where we had learned absolutely nothing, and most of all those warm, comfortable beds, where seven or eight boys would bundle up under one blanket. It was almost as if Yusuf had given news of the savior's birth.

CHAPTER 8

GOODBYE, ANTOURA

THE CLOUDS SEEMED like a permanent fixture in the sky, and torrential rain poured down for days on end. We stayed in the cave and shivered. On the third night after our last raid, we couldn't wait any longer. We decided to leave that evening.

As night fell, our eyes were glued on Yusuf, who would give the final order to move out. Strangely, we were all moved, now that we knew we would leave our third and final domicile in the mountains.

Yusuf led our motley column, followed closely by Murad, then Nishan, then Kevork, and at the very rear, me, trying my best to follow Kevork's exact footsteps. As we walked, we passed our second cave, which had sheltered us for many months. Outside were traces of a bonfire and the remnants of a feast, as well as empty bottles. Clearly, some villagers had spent a night there, having a great time.

We later passed by our first cave, where we had stayed for just a few days. We saw large amounts of animal dung and figured that some shepherd had probably taken shelter there, alongside his flock, probably trying to escape the fury of the rainstorms.

We also saw many lights on the hillsides and down in the valley. We could even hear the dogs of the villages barking.

We began our descent. We passed Father Francis's home, then the "big house," then the "small house." Finally, we spotted the familiar lights of the orphanage.

On Yusuf's order, we paused near the "small house." "Wait for me here, I'll be right back," he said before heading into the darkness toward Father Francis's orchard. Within an hour, he ran back to us with two bags full of apples and pears. We walked through the cemetery. We didn't see any body parts littering the floor, nor did we notice any new mounds of dirt, which meant that there had not been any recent casualties at the orphanage. We breathed a sigh of relief and proceeded toward the outer wall of the orphanage.

We climbed over the wall behind the chapel and dropped into the courtyard. There were no guards. Were they all asleep? Had boys stopped escaping? We walked toward the gymnasium—still, no guards anywhere. Yusuf hid the two bags of fruit behind some rocks.

As dawn broke, we tiptoed up the stairs into our dormitories. An eerie silence greeted us.

It had been almost six months since we had been in a bed. We each climbed into a random bed, without giving heed to who was beside us, and burrowed under the blankets. In the morning, I would have to explain myself, but that could wait a few hours. For the first time in months, I slept peacefully.

In the morning, as soon as I opened my eyes, I became aware that all around me were boys conversing in Armenian. What had happened here?

I recognized the boy lying beside me in the bed. He stared at me in utter shock.

"Where have you been? Where did you live? How did you survive? How come you're not dead?" He kept pelting me with questions.

In a few words, I summarized how we had lived in the wilderness. It was now his turn to explain.

"The soldiers left yesterday! Today the headmaster and teachers are leaving, too. Starting tomorrow, there will be no Turks at the orphanage!" he exclaimed.

"Where did they go? Where are they going?" I asked, scarcely believing my ears.

"Who knows? But they're not here anymore!" he replied.

"What's going to happen to all of us? Who's going to take care of us?"

"They said other people are coming, Armenian teachers and staff. Speaking Armenian will no longer be forbidden!" Indeed, Armenian kept pouring out of his lips.

Without anyone rushing them, the orphans made their way down to the courtyard. I could hear Armenian everywhere. With the freeing of their tongues, the boy's spirits were liberated. They played in the courtyard as boys do anywhere, without fear of punishment or furtive glances toward the supervising Turkish teachers.

Apparently, two days earlier, troops with wrapped heads and lances had come and taken away all the Turkish guards. Now the teachers had to leave, too.

Some of the older boys said that the war was over: the Turks had lost, and they were in full retreat back to their country.

Yusuf retrieved the stolen fruit from behind the rocks and distributed it to any boy that he came across. The boys devoured the large, juicy apples with relish, running all over the courtyard in euphoria.

There would be no more insults, no more beatings, no more endless lessons! It was a day of celebration!

Following the usual custom, we went down to the mess hall at eleven o'clock, without being hurried by the once-ubiquitous bell. The remaining staff served the usual gruel and the bun of bread, but they tasted delicious to me. The boys ate as if it were a feast, and Armenian names—not Turkish ones—were bandied across the table. These names had been buried deep in our hearts, and they were now being resurrected.

The Turkish women watched us eat with angry, vengeful expressions.

When we left the mess hall and returned to the courtyard, we could see the teachers, all lined up under a wall, their suitcases and bags beside them. They were talking among themselves, giving no heed to any of us. Nor did we care about their fates.

One of the teachers, however, noticed me, and approached my group of boys. She addressed me: "You! You've reappeared! Where have you been?"

"I was in the mountains," I answered.

"Mountains? What mountains? What were you doing there?"

"I was going to die of hunger here. My friends and I lived in the mountains and found a lot of fruit. We were never hungry up there."

"If you want to live so badly, why don't you come and be my son?" she smiled to me and stroked my hair.

I wouldn't think of it! "No! I want to stay with my friends!"

A few of the older boys loaded the teachers' baggage into the back of a waiting truck. The teachers climbed aboard. Within seconds, they were a speck in the distance.

We had been saved. The Armenian orphans had been returned to their nation.

ᴗ

As soon as the orphanage staff disappeared, the town's butcher and a few storeowners paid us a visit. They headed straight for the small barn that was in one corner of the grounds and drove away two cows and a horse, showering us with oaths on their way out. The reason for their pitiless behavior was clear: the orphanage owed them a lot of money.

Following their example, the boys immediately went to work. They attacked the orphanage's garden, violently stripping the soil of any vegetables and plucking the trees of all their fruit. They didn't even bother washing them; they simply devoured them on the spot.

The only staff left at the orphanage was the hapless Shukri, the quartermaster and a local. But he had no authority over the boys. So absolute chaos erupted. There was nobody to impose order, nobody to stop hundreds upon hundreds of hungry boys from rampaging through the place, gobbling up every scrap of food.

As dinnertime came and went, the boys realized that there was nobody to feed them. They had to fend for themselves, so they continued acting like a mad mob.

Kevork, Nishan, and I huddled in a corner, watching this spectacle of gluttony and hunger. At about dinnertime, Yusuf came over and gave us each a couple of apples. All around us were boys munching on whatever they could find. There was no punishment to fear; there was nobody to mete out punishment. But there was nobody to give us bread, either.

Then, in the evening, a few trucks screeched to a halt right outside the gates. About a dozen women and men emerged from the first truck, and a large group of women, young and old, came off the second truck. They were all speaking Armenian.

Hundreds of us gathered at the closed gate. Looking pitiful in our torn, discolored, ancient uniforms, we gaped at the well-dressed, well-mannered strangers who were clearly Armenian. Our language sounded so sonorous when uttered by these nice people!

The newcomers came inside. They began stroking our hair and kissing us, just like our fathers and mothers would have done had they found us after all this time.

At first, they asked the boys when and how they had lost their parents, but the reawakening of such bitter memories caused consternation among the orphans. Some broke into tears. The newcomers realized the mistake, and they started steering the conversation in more cheerful directions.

Shukri guided the new staff to the administration building. Some of the older boys followed, carrying the bags and suitcases.

Soon, some of the women headed down into the mess hall, while some of the men went into town and returned with several full bags of supplies. The bell rang, and just as before we lined up quietly and prepared for dinner. When we took our seats, we saw the same old bowls and the same old utensils, but inside the bowls were huge pieces of freshly baked bread, a large slice of cheese, and a dozen olives.

"Please be content with what we have tonight," said one of the women, as she went from table to table. "Tonight we'll only have dry bread, cheese, and olives, with warm milk, but starting tomorrow, I promise you, you'll have three meals a day—hot meals—and you'll often have meat. Thank you for your patience, boys."

She didn't realize that this meal was probably the best any of us had had for several years.

"Drip the bread into your milk, it makes it better!" the women suggested, fretting over us with motherly care.

All around me were figures of authority speaking in Armenian. I couldn't believe my ears. And when I looked down at my bowl, I couldn't believe my eyes, either. I had not seen bread of this size for years. We would actually leave the mess hall with our bellies full! It was a miracle! I had thought that we were returning to our old hell, but instead we'd found a new heaven.

We left the mess hall under the watchful, loving eyes of the Armenian women. Suddenly, the burden of being orphans had become lighter on our shoulders. We were now surrounded by love—motherly, unconditional love. We no longer felt alone, and the instinct to steal disappeared. We no longer had to resort to theft to supplement our meager diets. We once again felt like a part of humanity, a part of the Armenian nation.

The new staff members started to register the orphans, according to their Armenian names and their places of origin. The older boys had not forgotten their names or the names of their parents, but some of the younger ones had trouble remembering. In cases where it was impossible to verify the boys' names, they were assigned new Armenian names.

Our Turkish names were immediately forgotten. The küçük beys cast off their wolf's clothing; they became sheep again. Now Little Talaat, Little Enver, and Little Jemal again called themselves Toros, Mgrdich, and Dikran, and they played with the rest of the boys as if nothing unpleasant had ever happened. The days of their power were now over. We were all equal now, without exception.

One boy from Marash, who had become completely Turkified, did his best to atone for his sins by relearning Armenian and constantly insulting the Turkish language and the old Turkish staff. Unfortunately, he was not forgiven. He had sold out his own brothers for the sake of an extra bun of bread or bowl of gruel, and he paid for his crimes with his life. One morning, his body was found right outside the walls, beaten beyond recognition. Nobody ever knew what had happened to him or who had killed him. He was buried in the cemetery and left to the jackals.

An investigation was launched and inquiries were made, but they resulted in nothing, and the event was soon forgotten. In the eyes of the boys, he had committed the worst of crimes—betrayal. He served as an example for the rest of us: he put his interests above those of all the others, and he caused pain to his kind for insignificant material gain. As a result, he was killed, buried alone, and quickly forgotten. Nobody mourned him.

The entire atmosphere at the orphanage was transformed. Barbers from the village gave haircuts to all of the orphans, and they rubbed our heads with a strange, foul-smelling liquid. We also took a bath—the first bath we'd had in years—and received clean underwear and clothes. The cotton felt so pleasant against our bodies. We wore pressed pants, shorts, and long-sleeved sweaters. We had clean socks and a new, proper pair of shoes, which many of the boys had trouble walking in—they had become accustomed to bare feet.

Some of the boys sauntered about clicking their heels, feeling superior in their fancy clothing. Many of them had never dressed so well, not even back home. Others complained to the teachers and asked to be allowed to go barefoot. "Don't worry, my boy, keep wearing your shoes and soon you'll get used to them." They took the boys' hands and helped them walk up and down the courtyard.

We received three meals each day—breakfast, lunch, and dinner. On the third day, our lunch and dinner was potato stew with meat. It was the first meat we had tasted since we had entered the orphanage.

The head of the new administration, who was called Abu Nasif, often appeared in the courtyard. He had salt-and-pepper hair and a beard, wore large glasses, and walked with a military gait. He often participated in the boys' games, exhibiting the agility and speed of a much younger man. He astounded the orphans. No older man had ever taken part in their games.

After five or six days, we had to line up in the courtyard in our new clothes. We were returning to classes. The teachers ushered us inside with serious expressions, but there were no more insults, no more abuse, no more hitting with sticks or the falakha. Not even strikes of the ruler!

From that first day, all subjects were taught in Armenian. Because we came from different areas, we had a litany of accents and spoke a number of

Armenian dialects, so at first it was difficult to pinpoint exactly how much we knew and how much we needed to learn.

They gave each of us an Armenian primer, which we were supposed to read in our free time. We stared at the letters and the pictures, understanding very little. I remembered my similar book when I'd gone to school in Gurin. My mother had brought that primer with us all the way to Hama, hoping I'd resume my interrupted education. God knows what happened to that book. But now I had a new one, and although I still didn't recognize the letters, they felt relatively familiar to me.

It took us only a few months to begin reading entire words. We were young, and our minds were receptive to lessons that we cared about.

They also started teaching us Armenian hymns, poems, and songs, which we sang in our classes, during recesses, and even to ourselves in our dormitories. We could now recite the Hayr Mer and poems such as *Azad Asdvadz* correctly, and we could sing the Armenian national anthem, as well as hymns like *Aravod Louso*.

In history class, we learned the story of Hayg killing Pel, the creation myth of the Armenian nation. We learned that Armenia had once been a powerful nation, and that it would rise up once again from the ashes.

Before our meals, we recited the Hayr Mer and crossed ourselves. Only then did we eat. The bowls and the plates were always full. A mound of bread rose from each table. We no longer rushed to eat, no longer grabbed food out of each other's grasp.

On New Year's Eve, the staff organized a celebration. There were delicacies, songs, a beautiful dance performed by one of the teachers, and even a visit from Santa Claus. He gave us all stockings full of confections, raisins, walnuts, almonds, and dried fruit. There was no limit to the orphans' joy. We remembered how back home, on New Year's Day, we would go from home to home, gathering gifts. Those old, happy days seemed to be coming back.

One day, several trucks stopped right outside the gate, and troops poured out of them. These were all Armenian soldiers[*] and they ran into

---

[*] These were soldiers of the Armenian Legion, a unit of Armenian soldiers armed and trained by the French military.

the courtyard, embracing the orphans and lifting them into the air. They acted as if they had found their own long-lost sons. They were dressed in impeccably clean uniforms and boots and wore long, pointy hats. A few had medals on their chests, and some even had one, two, or three yellow stripes sewn on the arms of their uniforms, depending on their rank. They were young and healthy, and their presence was a cause for celebration in the orphanage. They couldn't be any more different from the Turkish troops they had replaced.

Soldiers visited us on a weekly basis. One Sunday, more than five hundred of them came! And they came just to see us, the orphans of their crucified nation. They stayed all day, and at noon they ate with us in the mess hall. It was an intriguing experience for the boys, breaking bread with these Armenian troops in gleaming uniforms and medals.

After lunch, some soldiers gave speeches. They said we would all go to Cilicia and rebuild Armenia. There was no end to the cheers and the applause.

Some of the teachers and staff members gave speeches, too. The whole day was spent in high spirits, amid speeches, songs, and good wishes. At night, the soldiers kissed us, promised to meet us again in Cilicia, and left us in a dreamy, euphoric state.

For days after the troops' departure, the boys didn't speak of anything else. Everyone talked of Cilicia, of the new Armenia, and of finding the soldiers once we got there.

The happiest among the boys, of course, were those who were natives of Cilicia—those who had been deported from cities and towns like Adana, Hajin, Zeytun, Marash, and Aintab. These boys knew that they would return to their old homelands.

One Saturday, the chapel was finally opened. Some of the staff members washed and cleaned the interior, and with the help of some local villagers they raised the statue and put it back on its plinth. Fortunately, the altar and stained glass windows were intact.

That Sunday, all the orphans, regardless of age, were led to the chapel. Near the altar, some of the teachers, alongside some of the teenage orphans, had formed a choir and sang otherworldly hymns. We listened in reverence, occasionally crossing ourselves. The choir reminded me of the church we used to attend in Gurin, bringing tears to my eyes.

Winter came, and we spent it mostly studying. We learned how to read, how to write, how to add and subtract. We learned Armenian history, which was probably our favorite class, mostly because we learned about the heroic deeds of brave kings and queens, stories that excited our imagination and filled us with an awareness of what Armenia had been and could once again become.

We were proud of our accomplishments, achieved in such a short time. By spring, the older boys were already learning poetry. It was a miraculous transformation—we were becoming educated young men.

The school year concluded with a large celebration in the chapel. Our teachers gave passionate speeches, promising us again that we would soon all be back in Armenia. The older boys recited poetry and sang patriotic songs. Afterward, when we poured out into the courtyard, the celebrations continued. An almost hysterical intoxication had overwhelmed the orphans.

"We're going back home! We're going back to Armenia!" we shouted.

"I'll go straight back to Adana!" exclaimed Yusuf.

"We'll be going back to Sepastia!" said the three brothers Hovhannes, Boghos, and Kalust.

"We'll be returning to Sis!" proclaimed Nishan and Kevork.

"I'll soon be in Gurin!" I thought. I wondered whether I would find Krikor there.

We orphans were remnants of a vast nation. We constituted the new generation of Armenians. We didn't know what had happened to our families. Most of our homes probably had been razed to the ground or taken over by Turks or Kurds.

Many of my family members had died in the concentration camp. What had happened to the rest? Where were they now? I wondered, too, about my fate and my old home. Would I ever get back to Gurin? Would our house still be standing? Would the door be open or locked?

I forced myself out of these daydreams. My friends were playing nearby. I joined their games, but my mind kept drifting back into the past and forward into the future. Would I really be back home soon, in the bosom of what remained of my family?

That evening's dinner was sumptuous. We were served delicious rice pudding and warm loaves of bread. For the first time in years, I couldn't finish a meal.

After dinner, we were taken into the gymnasium. It was our first time in this hall. Although covered, it was well-illuminated, with windows that opened to the west. Abu Nasif climbed onto the stage, alongside a teacher named Mr. Melkon. Abu Nasif spoke in a fatherly tone, the Arabic words flowing from his mouth, while Mr. Melkon translated for the orphans. "Boys, in two weeks you will leave the orphanage and will make your way to Cilicia. You will not be alone. We will accompany you along the way, and when we finally get there, your life as orphans will come to an end. You now have your own government, which will take care of you. You will go to school, and when you're done you will go to university to study. You will become doctors, chemists, and engineers. Some of you may even become veterinarians!"

After his speech, Abu Nasif closed his eyes and said a short prayer, asking God to watch over us orphans and protect us from evil.

The orphans exchanged awed glances as they left the gymnasium. We had been in an orphanage that didn't even have a doctor on its staff. Many had died simply because there had been no medical help, no medicine, no adequate nurses. And now we learned that there were future doctors in our ranks!

"Abu Nasif said we'd become doctors, engineers, and veterinarians, but he said nothing about us becoming soldiers! We'll be soldiers, too, even generals!" said Nishan. Many of the boys agreed with him. For years, they had nurtured a deadly hatred of the Turks, and they thought the best way to exact revenge was to become soldiers and fight the enemy on the battlefield.

"Once we get to Cilicia, we won't leave a single Turk alive!" added

Murad. Others, too, thundered and stormed against the Turks, listing all the things they'd do if they caught a Turk alive back home.

Two weeks passed like two years. Every morning, the boys woke up with new dreams. There was an extraordinary desire to get to Cilicia as quickly as possible.

One morning, some local priests came to the orphanage. They held a meeting with Abu Nasif and then went all around the institution, examining various rooms, and praying in the chapel. When they left the chapel, their eyes immediately went to the roof, where the statues of saints had once stood. The priests spoke in hushed tones and shook their heads in dismay. When we left, these priests would turn the orphanage back into a monastery.

Finally, the day of departure came. The orphans lined up quietly and were led down into the courtyard by the teachers. Almost four years earlier we had entered through those gates, and since then we had been prisoners. For four years we had suffered from beatings and hunger. A few hundred of us had died.

Now we left through those same gates. We mounted trucks, and within minutes, without any unnecessary farewells, we were moving, leaving the orphanage behind. After a few bends in the road, Antoura was no longer visible. We cursed the place under our breath.

On the way, each truckload of boys was given some bread, which we shared equitably and ate happily. The locals had come outside, greeting us, waving to us, and wishing us the best. Some of the older men appeared with baskets of apples, which they distributed to the boys. These were the same villagers whose gardens we had robbed mercilessly, but these kind people had forgiven us. Old women lined the way, crossing themselves and blessing us with tears in their eyes.

We came to the village of Zouk. It seemed like its entire population had poured out into the streets to see our passage. They gave us apples and pears and wished us a safe trip.

The winding road led us down to the coast. More people waved and wished us well from the side of the road. I was moved by the kindness of the locals, who themselves were Christians and had suffered under the rule of the Turks.

Finally, we spotted the sea—the endless, blue sea. We had reached Beirut, from where we would depart for Cilicia.

Goodbye Antoura! We were headed back home! Back to our towns and our families!

Karnig Panian with his family, (*left to right*) daughter Chaghik, Karnig, wife Araxie, daughter Houry, 1954.

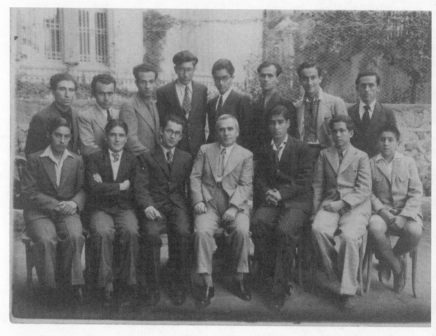

Karnig Panian (*standing second from left*) with teacher Karnig Guzelian (*seated in center*) and the first students admitted to the newly opened Hamazkayin Djemaran (High School) in Beirut, early 1930s.

Karnig Panian (*second row, seated fourth from right*) with colleagues and students of the Hamazkayin Djemaran (High School) in Beirut, 1951. Levon Shant, principal of the school and founder of the Hamazkayin Educational and Cultural Society, is at the center of the group (*standing ninth from the left*).

(*Left to right*) Karnig Panian, with leading Armenian public figures Garo Sassouni, Simon Vratsian (prime minister of Armenia during the First Republic), and Vahan Papazian, late 1950s.

Karnig Panian (*second from right*) with members of the central board of the
Hamazkayin Educational and Cultural Association next to the newly erected bust of
Nigol Aghpalian, early 1960s. Aghpalian was a member of the Armenian parliament
and appointed minister of education in 1919. He founded, with Levon Shant, the
Hamazkayin Djemaran (High School) in Beirut in 1928.

Karnig Panian (*third from left*) at the historic meeting of His Holiness Vasken I and His Holiness Khoren I in Jerusalem, 1963.

Karnig Panian receiving the Mesrob Mashdots Medal from His Holiness Khoren I, 1970. The Mesrob Mashdots Medal is the highest honor given to intellectuals and educators by the Holy See of Cilicia.

Karnig Panian surrounded by his family, Lebanon, 1986. (*Left to right*)
Grandchildren Annie, Haig, Steve; Karnig; grandchild Alik; wife Araxie; daughter
Houry; and grandchild Taline.

Karnig Panian's daughters and grandchildren, Lebanon, 1986. (*Left to right*) Grandchildren Annie, Haig; daughter Chaghik; grandchild Alik; daughter Houry; and grandchild Taline.

Cross-Stone (*Khatchkar*) erected at the Antoura College in 2010 in memory of the orphans who perished at the orphanage of Antoura.

Source: Photo by Missak Kelechian. Reprinted by permission.

CHAPTER 9

SONS OF A GREAT NATION

OUR TRAIN OUT OF BEIRUT chugged along, whistling as it climbed the mountains. New summits kept appearing in the dark distance. We were restless, crammed into the wagons, whiling away the time with pranks and jokes while dreaming of Cilicia.

As the train descended from the highlands, we saw boundless vineyards on both sides of the tracks. We gaped out the window, marveling at vines as far as the eye could see, heavy with succulent grapes. Going through these fields, I was reminded of home, of our bountiful Tsakh Tsor with its orchards of berries, apricots, and plums. It almost seemed like we were going back home.

But then came the call of the conductor—*Hama! Hama!* And the train screeched to a halt in a familiar station.

I stared at the caves near our old camp. That was where my village had lost most of its sons and daughters. In those caves and on those sands, under the searing sun, thousands had died of hunger and of disease, including most of my extended family. That was where I might have died, too, if my grandparents had not taken me to the orphanage at Hama. But since Jemal Pasha had ordered us to Antoura, I had lost contact with my family. I never discovered what had happened to my grandmother, grandfather, aunt, and cousins. Nor did I know Krikor's fate after he escaped the orphanage.

Had they joined the long procession of the dead? I had no idea, and I had no way of finding out.

The caves sent terrible memories rushing back to me. In a single moment, I relived those months of horrible suffering in the desert. My gaze remained glued to where the camp had stood, and tears gushed from my eyes.

Finally, the train whistled and chugged forward. The orphans were excited to reach Cilicia, and I eventually gave in and joined the merriment, though I couldn't shake off the shock of seeing Hama again.

Occasionally, when we passed farms, the field hands, who were mostly boys about our age, would wave at us. We'd respond in kind, glad to make a human connection with someone from the outside world. We felt strangely akin to those boys, as if we had always been friends.

Sometimes, when the train stopped at a station, locals would climb on with baskets full of food and snacks. Unfortunately, none of us had any money, so the merchants always left empty-handed.

After four or five hours, we arrived in Aleppo. We were told to disembark, and the train soon whistled and sped away, leaving us on the station platform.

Abu Nasif and the teachers led us toward a small circle of tents that had been pitched outside the station. We followed without a word. We were staying here for a week or two because the facilities in Cilicia were not yet ready to accept us. It was almost dark when we wearily settled into our tents. Kind folks from the city soon arrived, bearing bags of bread, cheese pastries, and canned goods.

Every day that we were in Aleppo dozens of Armenians came to our improvised campsite in the hopes of finding a relative. Some did find long-lost loved ones, and their outbursts of joy often left them hysterical and in tears.

One day, my aunt Hnazant appeared at the camp, alongside her two sons, Krikor and Ardashes. She threw her arms around me and sobbed for a long time. She could barely say a word. Krikor, stolid as usual, told me of his adventures since our separation, beginning with his escape from Antoura and continuing with the tale of how he found his mother and brother.

Ardashes, meanwhile, remained silent, staring at me awkwardly. We had both grown older by four years since we had last seen each other. He was still trying to overcome the shock of seeing me alive after all that time.

Eventually, after calming down, my aunt explained to me that their plan was to head to Aintab, and she advised me to follow them there.

The committee in charge of the transient orphans made two separate lists of the boys, depending on their preferred destination within Cilicia. Most wanted to go to the city of Adana, but I was among those who chose Aintab, since I would be among family there. I would live in an orphanage, but knowing that I would have relatives nearby gave me a measure of strength.

One day, the orphans leaving for Adana were told to pack their belongings, and they soon parted from us. Two days later, a train pulled into the station to take the rest of us to Aintab. We finally headed out of Aleppo. At the next station, a dozen French military transport trucks were parked outside, waiting for our arrival. Among the many French soldiers were a few Armenians. These men kindly helped us into the trucks. We passed through Kilis, where we had once stopped during our forced march to Hama, and proceeded toward Aintab.

The road was bumpy. Inside the uncomfortable trucks we struggled to keep ourselves from falling onto each other. On both sides, the road was lined with trees. The boys were excited, especially those from this region. Finally, in a valley ahead, we spotted the woods of Ghavakhlikh,* and then, beyond them, the city of Aintab, flowing down the flanks of the mountains and into the flatlands.

"That's Aintab! That's Aintab!" The locals couldn't contain their excitement. After all these years, they were returning to the city they called home.

"Our house is right downtown," said the boy next to me. "It's a big one. In fact, I think we're heading right for it!"

The trucks rolled down deserted, winding roads toward the heart of Aintab. The roads were lined with small, one-story homes, though occasionally we spied some taller buildings. The steeple of the church, with

---

* Ghavakhlikh is Kavaklık, now a neighborhood within Gaziantep.

the cross at its peak, was hard to spot among the many roofs, though the minarets of mosques majestically rose toward the skies. The Armenian neighborhoods of the city were eerily empty. Now and then, we saw some-one exiting a home. We also saw a few people repairing homes that had recently been damaged. There were many turbaned men walking among these Armenians, glaring at them with disdain, as if thinking, "Here are those damned bastards again."

The trucks slowly navigated the narrow roads of the city. They crawled as we reached large crowds in the Turkish parts of town. We saw women with their faces veiled. Urchins ran around in their bare feet. Men in *shalvars*—large baggy trousers—appeared here and there, some turbaned, almost all fiddling with their prayer beads.

We passed a variety of shops, including a barber, cobbler, coppersmith, and baker. The delectable aroma of warm bread and fresh cakes filled the air. It reminded me of our market back home.

The trucks, winding through the crowds and honking constantly, finally approached a large building with an arched gate. They drove right through it without even slowing down.

The trucks came to a halt in a vast courtyard. We stepped down, and immediately the teachers began reading our names and grouping us by class. Because most of the boys in my class had chosen to go to Adana, only ten of us were left. Once we were lined up, the teachers led us to the second floor of the building. There were already other boys there who oc-cupied most of the rooms we passed. They silently glared at us as we walked through the hallways, though we soon began to fraternize.

Our beds were mats laid out on the floor, covered in thick, warm blan-kets. There was no other furniture in our rooms. When the bell rang, we lined up and walked into a large mess hall. There were no tables, only mats covering the floor. Plates were arranged in semi-circles for each classroom. The boys each took a seat behind a plate and recited the Hayr Mer. Then the caretakers filled our plates with generous helpings of meat and potatoes, and each boy also received some bread, which reminded me of the bread from the end of our time in the Antoura orphanage—soft, creamy, and delicious.

We ate with relish, and then, to our delight, we each received a bunch of grapes to top off the meal. After we all finished eating, we once again prayed.

The facility was huge. In its enormous courtyard a hundred boys could play comfortably at the same time. The first floor had about thirty rooms, with windows facing the courtyard. Most of the rooms on the first floor were reserved for livestock, while the others served as storage. The rooms on the second floor, however, were bedrooms, and the mess hall was on that floor as well. Clearly, this building had once been a caravansary.

The next day, a small group of men came to visit us. They were Armenians who had converted to Islam, and they were trying to find long-lost relatives or friends. They seemed meek and subservient, carrying the guilt of apostates upon their shoulders. Most of the orphans, by contrast, were more brazen about their Armenian identity and native tongue.

Our new home was called Millet Khan, and it was located in a neighborhood known for its rabidly fanatical Turkish population. We had come all this way, yet we still faced the prejudice of the Turks. Whenever we were outside the orphanage, we felt a hundred hateful eyes upon us, and we lived in constant fear.

Three days after our arrival in Aintab, we began our classes. Our teachers were all Armenian, and most of them had come with us from Antoura. We sat on mats on the floor, holding our books and notebooks against our knees. We didn't even have blackboards. But there was a high priority placed on Armenian language and Armenian history.

Given our deprivations, we held education in high regard. Moreover, we no longer had to learn on empty stomachs, as we did in Antoura. Well-fed boys make good students.

In Aintab, we ate three meals a day, every day, and the food was always plentiful. We also bathed with hot water once a week, which we very much appreciated. In Antoura, we had bathed perhaps four times in four years.

Soon, we could read and write rather well, and our vocabulary grew more prolific. Even in the courtyard, during recess, we read aloud to each other, though we were not allowed to sing aloud. We were in a Turkish neighborhood, after all. "If you sing, boys, do it softly!" the teachers would exhort us. "They may hear you. Then there'll be arguments and fights!"

"But we can barely hear ourselves sing!," we protested.

"Well, turn it down a little bit more," they replied. "Some day, you'll be able to sing as loud as you want."

༒

The Great War was long over, and Turkey had lost. As Armenians returned to the homes they had left behind, they still felt unsafe within the confines of Turkey.

We now had a new headmaster, a colossal American man named Ray Travis.* He had a bright smile, blond hair, and penetrating eyes, and when he walked it was as if the earth shook beneath his feet. But this giant of a man had a soft, gentle soul. He would chat with us, crack jokes, and take part in our games. He loved us with all his heart, and he soon gained our confidence and friendship, becoming a surrogate father to us all.

Mr. Travis often ate with us in the mess hall instead of dining separately with the rest of the faculty. Before our meals, he prayed in English, but he never crossed himself at the end of the prayers. We found this extremely odd until we learned that he was a Protestant. I didn't care about his religion. What mattered to me was that he was a kind, loving man.

During the day, he was almost always with us. At night, he looked into our bedrooms, covering the boys who had kicked off their blankets in their sleep. He often appeared in the classrooms, and he made sure we were clean and well groomed. He even tasted all of the food before it was served to us, ensuring that it was up to his standards.

Toward the end of the school year, our class had gone through the entire Armenian textbook, and I could read fluently. I often entertained my friends by reciting stories from the textbook. They were amazed at my abil-

---

* Ray P. Travis was a missionary and civil servant; he served in World War I, in France, then undertook relief work as a missionary in Aintab and later became director of the Near East Relief orphanage in Jubayl, Lebanon.

ity to absorb and retain information. One day, one of them looked at me and prophetically stated, "Just you wait, you'll be a teacher someday!"

One morning in the spring of 1920, the teachers woke us up early. "We're going to the Armenian quarter of the city," they explained.

Unsure what was happening, we lined up by class behind our teachers and hurried down the stairs. We found Mr. Travis waiting for us, holding a large American flag in his hands. We filed behind the headmaster, who raised the flag high and led us onto the city streets.

The sun had not yet risen when our procession left the gates of the orphanage. The streets were still deserted and silent. Stray dogs scampered about, occasionally barking, and we heard the crowing of roosters. Some locals stuck their heads out of their windows and watched us pass in amazement.

A few early risers had gathered to enjoy breakfast at a bakery. "Where are you boys headed?" asked some Armenians, but their inquiries received no reply.

"We're in the Armenian quarter of Aintab!" finally announced our teacher, Mr. Melkon. The orphans stared around them but kept up their pace, as if scared to be in the neighborhood.

To our left we saw the steeple of a church. It was proof that, indeed, we were in an Armenian neighborhood. A bakery displayed its goods on a rock outside the store. A cobbler was already hard at work. The street was coming to life around us, the shops opening their shutters one by one. Everybody was speaking Armenian. We were among our own kind. We proceeded down some winding roads and climbed a small hill that overlooked the city. Finally, our headmaster stopped in front of a large facility, which we later learned had once been Shepard Hospital.*

Mr. Travis planted the flag in the ground and turned to face us. "From now on, we will all live in these buildings," he said. "You will all be safe here,

---

* Shepard Hospital was named after Dr. Fred Douglas Shepard, 1855–1915, a missionary who worked at Azariah Smith Medical Hospital attached to Central Turkey College in Aintab. Shepard attempted to save the Armenians from deportations and massacre, even traveling to Constantinople to that end. He contracted typhus from Armenian deportees and died on December 18, 1915, in Aintab.

and you will be able to work and play freely." For the first time, I grasped
how unsafe we had been in the Turkish neighborhood.

Two days later, the situation became much worse. Violence broke out
around the Armenian quarter. Turks began indiscriminately shooting in the
general direction of Armenian homes and neighborhoods. We had barely
settled down in our new orphanage when we heard multiple shots close to
the buildings.

"Help! Help! My wife! Help me!" screamed a local man. His wife lay
motionless on the ground. Nobody knew who had shot her.

"Stay away from the windows!" called out the teachers. "Keep your
heads down and stay on the floor!"

It was too late. A bullet pierced a window and struck an orphan named
Manug. He was fifteen years old, from Adana. He was a healthy boy until
his life was cut short in an instant.

Mr. Travis ordered the cobblestones in the courtyard to be dug up and
used to barricade the windows. We found some picks and shovels, and our
teachers rolled up their sleeves and went to work. Within two or three
hours the windows were completely barricaded, and not a moment too
soon; the shooting was getting worse. Terrified Armenians, hoping that the
American flag outside would afford them some protection, began crowding
into the orphanage.

Mr. Travis ran back and forth, making arrangements and settling disputes. He had a few of the boys following him. At one point, they left
and reappeared a few hours later, having procured weapons and ammunition from the French troops stationed nearby. They distributed the weapons
among young men in the crowd, stationing them at strategic spots around
the hospital building. They were ordered to fire without pause.

"Let the Turks know that we are not unarmed, that we will fight fire
with fire!" declared Mr. Travis, as if he himself were Armenian.

The terrified women and children stayed with the orphans while the
men spread out with their weapons. Even the old men joined the fray.
Outside, the exchange of fire kept going. The Armenians set up barricades
around the orphanage and prepared for the worst.

We orphans had come here with dreams of returning to our homes and families, but now we found ourselves once again in the midst of violence, though still too young and inexperienced to carry weapons and join the fight.

Rumors spread that many Armenians had come from the surrounding towns to join the fighters in Aintab. We heard that there was an established military committee, giving orders and supervising the Armenian forces. All of the Armenian neighborhoods in town had been become battlefields.

Mr. Travis seemed to be everywhere. From his flat on the upper floor of the hospital, he constantly sniped in the direction of the Turkish mobs. At other times, he was down on the barricades, rallying the people, exhorting them to keep on fighting.

Our orphanage had become a fort, offering sanctuary to almost the entire Armenian population of Aintab. The administration announced a rationing system. All food would be shared with the community. Now, for lunch, we received a large spoonful of wheat pilaf, some bread, and a piece of cheese. For dinner, all we ate was bread and cheese. The rationing reminded us of the Antoura orphanage, though the bread was bigger and better than the rock-hard, walnut-sized buns of Antoura.

A mosque was adjacent to the Armenian neighborhoods. From its minaret we usually heard the imam's calls to prayer. But for days we heard nothing. We learned that some Turks had fled out of fear of their proximity to the Armenians.

Armenians began making forays into the Turkish neighborhoods. They looted and set fire to homes and stores. Some of the loot was given to the orphanage administration and helped the Armenian refugees survive. One day, returning from a scavenging trip to the nearby Turkish neighborhoods, men entered the orphanage with wheelbarrows full of flour, wheat, lentils, and other grains. We breathed a sigh of relief. We had food for a while, and we didn't worry too much about where it all came from.

We were accustomed to hunger, but that didn't mean we didn't desperately want to go to sleep with full bellies. We had to live somehow. We had starved and stolen and foraged, and those memories constantly haunted us. We never wanted to sink that low again.

꙳

Near Shepard Hospital was the Halajian School, which had also once served as an orphanage. It had a wide, clean courtyard. Whenever there was a lull in the shooting, we orphans would go out there and play. It was a risky thing, and as soon as we heard shots again, we would flee back to our building.

One day, we were playing in the courtyard when a shell landed nearby and exploded with a deafening boom. A stampede ensued, as we all ran to the doors in absolute panic. Fortunately, none of the boys were close enough to get hurt.

That shell was followed by a constant bombardment of the area. It was imperative to move people out of the danger zone. Our leaders decided that the safest place for us was an underground cave beneath the Halajian School. We orphans had not even known about the cave's existence.

All of the orphans, along with many families that had been taking shelter in the orphanage, went down to the cave. It was dark, but it was quite roomy—at least twenty-five meters long and fifteen meters wide. A makeshift door had been installed at its entrance, and a few narrow windows carved out of the rock allowed for light and air. I was assigned a place right near the door, underneath one of those narrow windows. I had a single blanket, which I mostly used to shelter myself from the hot rays of the morning sun.

We endured intense mental stress in that cave. Most of the women and children had to worry not only about themselves, but also about the men who fought the Turks in the city above. Every morning, there was utter chaos—the cries and complaints of the infants, the exhortations of the mothers, the laughter and games of the orphans.

Two or three times a day women bearing baskets of bread and cheese would come to the cave. Each of us received one bun. We orphans could handle it, but the women and children with us had trouble adjusting to the meager rations.

As the days passed, the fighting seemed to intensify. The Turkish mob kept attacking the Armenian positions. Our forces repelled them each time, yet the sounds of explosions seemed to be getting closer to our cave. Every day, our fighters would come and relay good news to us, keeping our spirits high.

One night we woke up to a terrible explosion that seemed to shake the earth beneath us. In the morning, we realized what had happened. We could not see the minaret of the mosque! The explosion had destroyed it completely. The cityscape looked entirely different. This act enraged the Turks. They tried to respond by setting the Armenian church on fire, but the men guarding it stood their ground.

In the three months since the fighting had started, the situation became grimmer. The cannons roared all night, bombarding the Armenian neighborhoods, spraying homes and stores with their deadly shrapnel. Food was becoming scarcer, and tighter rations were introduced. The specter of hunger once again hung over our heads. We now got a dry piece of bread for lunch, with no cheese. For dinner, we just got a cup of pistachios. Pistachios were great, but they couldn't replace bread.

Because we were born Armenian, we were enduring incredible hardships, and we were making massive sacrifices for each other. I was acutely aware of how difficult it was to be Armenian. For five years, I had been suffering for no other reason.

One morning, as the cannons fell silent, some of us slipped outside. Still keeping our heads low, we went out into the open air. It was a beautiful day. The sun shone in the blue, cloudless sky.

"Relish these moments, boys, and remember them, because in a few minutes we'll have to be back in that damned cave," said one of the older boys.

"I think we're going to have bulgur pilaf for lunch. I can smell it all the way from here, I'm so hungry," added another.

"I wonder what we'll have for dinner."

"Haven't you all learned yet? We survived Antoura, now we'll have to survive Aintab. We'll survive on those succulent pistachios."

Just then, several bullets whistled overhead. "Inside! Go back inside!" came the call. We all ran into the cave.

"Ha! Let them shoot all they want!" said one of the boys.

"They can't hit a wall!" joked another.

We had seen too much to be scared of death.

That night, a few of the young soldiers visited the cave to see their relatives. They told incredible stories about the events unfolding on the battlefield. The Turks, apparently, had begun panicking and shooting at their own forces. The men looked healthy and strong. They stayed for only a short while before kissing their relatives and returning to the barricades.

These men left a huge impression on me. In my young mind, I believed that every Armenian man was a great husband, father, and general.

As the battle turned in our favor, the Turks who lived close to the Armenian neighborhoods totally abandoned their homes, and now their stores supplied us with grain and meat. The threat of famine vanished for a while. For lunch, we now received full meals. For dinner, though, we still got only pistachios.

The situation on the battlefield was fluid. Each day brought news. Now we heard that the Turks had been joined by hundreds of members of armed gangs from surrounding villages.

Soon there was a second front, near the mountains. Turkish reinforcements were traveling to the city from that direction. The Armenian neighborhoods were caught between two battles, and the shelling and shooting reached new levels of intensity.

Because of the deteriorating situation, Mr. Travis made repeated visits to Aintab College, where the French forces were stationed. He procured more rifles and ammunition, which he distributed among the Armenian fighters. Sometimes, he was even able to procure hand grenades. There were rumors that he was also negotiating with the French for direct military assistance against the Turkish forces.

The French were worried about the intervention of the English, who had only recently evacuated the area. Turkey, a loser in the Great War, was again trying to assert its hegemony. Unable to match the French force's military capabilities, the Turks vented their rage on the Armenians.

By summer, the heat inside the cave became unbearable. It was impossible to sleep inside. Ignoring the bullets that whizzed over our heads, we spent most nights in the open air. Sometimes, as bullets flew and shells exploded, we retold our adventures during the years of deportations and massacres, talking until we slipped into slumber.

Then, one morning, we learned that the French were leaving Aintab. Delegations from the local Armenians begged them to change their mind. We feared what would happen once the French left. "Why did they come in the first place?" cried the locals. "Why did they help us? They gave us guns and hope, now they're abandoning us!"

We orphans were again in limbo, uncertain of our fate.

〰

One day, Mr. Travis told us that we were leaving the next morning for Beirut. We would ride on French trucks as the French military evacuated.

We bade farewell to Aintab. With the declaration of a temporary cease-fire, an eerie silence suffused the city. Dark-skinned soldiers[46*] on horseback escorted the trucks, which carried about fifty or sixty orphans. Sometimes, the trucks halted and waited for the horsemen to catch up. A huge cloud of dust hovered above the vehicles, making it virtually impossible to see anything on the sides of the road.

As we entered Kilis, I saw a lone tree on a small hill. It looked as if it stood there specifically to welcome visitors entering the city. The trucks rumbled on. The road became bumpier and dustier, the air barely breathable.

When the trucks stopped at a train station, we jumped down from the trucks and boarded the wagons. Mr. Travis ran around, ensuring that we were all settled and comfortable. Our bedrolls and bundles of clothing were all stored in a specially marked wagon. We each received a small sliver of cheese and a cucumber.

For the past five years, we had been moved across deserts and mountains, without a moment of rest, without a place to call home. Was this our fate? Were we to be moved like cattle from one place to another for the rest of our lives? Lost in these thoughts, I watched the countryside zooming

---

* Among the French forces were soldiers from France's West African colonies.

past the train. Goats grazed calmly while villagers worked in the fields. I felt a strong sense of empathy with these people. From the depths of my heart, I wanted them to prosper. I wanted no more orphans in the world, no more destitute children.

A large crowd gathered at the Aleppo train station. Many of them spoke Armenian. These men had a short discussion with Mr. Travis, and subsequently a bunch of teenage boys climbed into our wagons, accompanied by an adult who seemed to be their teacher. They were orphans, too, and they joined our ranks.

We crossed the desert, past that accursed city of Hama, and arrived in Baalbek. We no longer felt the desert's searing heat, and we no longer saw Turkish troops on guard. Soldiers wearing the ridged helmets of the French army patrolled Baalbek, their rifles hanging loosely from their shoulders. They had kind faces.

We continued on our way. We crossed a valley that looked much like Tsakh Tsor. There was no stream, but there were acres of fruit trees, endless fields of green, and industrious villagers harvesting their crops. It was a land of plenty, with people living in peace. They never worried about hunger here.

New vistas appeared on the horizon—vast chains of mountains, endless valleys, and dark gorges. Here and there, we spotted a column of smoke rising from a village. That smoke was another sign of prosperity and of life—they were baking bread!

Then the train headed into another valley, and we saw the glimmering sea. Beirut and its outskirts looked like a vast outgrowth on the surface of the earth. The train made one last wide turn and whistled as it pulled into a large station. Cries of delight rose from our wagons, and a stampede ensued toward the doors as we all tried to alight first.

Mr. Travis jumped onto the platform and gathered the other teachers around him. A few men greeted him. After a short conversation, our teachers led us into a large courtyard, where a line of tents had been pitched. We were taking temporary shelter in these tents until we could arrange a more permanent home. Eight to ten boys shared each tent.

We devoured an evening meal of pita bread, cheese, and apricots, and then we headed to the nearby beach, where small waves crashed against the rocks. We watched the little fish swimming in and out of little crevices, and we shrieked with delight as we chased the waves back into the sea.

We were in an area called Karantina, which was right by the water.[*] Thickets of trees dotted the landscape, and we played under their shade. But our teachers soon ensured that we were not wandering all day, doing nothing at all.

On the third day after our arrival, our teachers gathered groups of students around them and dispersed to different thickets. We didn't have textbooks yet, so our classes consisted mostly of our teachers' reading or reciting to us. These were primitive lessons, primarily designed to ensure that we didn't become accustomed to a life of idleness.

We were excited to learn again. We sat cross-legged in the shade of the trees, in a circle around our teachers. Sometimes we had trouble hearing the lectures, but we did our best to capture every word. We were thirsty for knowledge.

I developed an interest in mathematics, though we still did only addition and subtraction. After language class, as we picked up new words, we all tried to use them during our games. When our teachers recounted the great deeds of the Armenian kings of yore, I thought, "Where are these kings now? How have our people fallen on such hard times?"

We began to forget the terrible days of Antoura and Aintab, yet we wondered whether our good fortune would last. We were afraid we would suddenly wake up and realize it had all been a dream. But every day, we got bread and fresh vegetables, and sometimes meat. The terror of hunger was becoming only a memory.

We grew fascinated by the sea. The teachers promised to teach us how to swim, and on the first afternoon that we went to the beach, many of the older boys stripped and headed right into the water. I couldn't understand

---

[*] La Quarantaine, colloquially referred to as Karantina, is the site of a quarantine station for travelers built in the early nineteenth century. It is in northeastern Beirut, adjacent to the port of Beirut and west of the Beirut River.

why they didn't sink. The younger orphans stayed near the beach, wetting their feet in the crashing waves. The teachers went from one to the other, encouraging them all to venture into the water.

An older boy helped me by carrying me into the sea. At first, I panicked. A few times, I sank like lead, swallowing water as I opened my mouth in terror. But slowly I got accustomed to it. Within a week or two, I was swimming like a fish.

I saw a complete transformation in us. Thanks to the exhortations of Mr. Travis and the faculty, even the most fearful of us had gone into the sea and overcome our anxiety. Everyone was now having fun, splashing around and exploring their newfound mastery over the waters.

Two weeks passed, and we were still living in the tents, eating and learning and swimming. Some new teachers joined us, raising the number of the faculty to fifteen. Each teacher had to teach only one or two subjects, though still with primitive supplies and without books.

We now had dedicated timeslots for calisthenics and military drills. Calisthenics was taught by Mr. Kopernik, while our drill instructor was Mr. Stepan. The latter seemed to think that we were really soldiers, and he would bark out martial orders in both Armenian and French. When one of us made a mistake during his classes, Mr. Stepan would lash out at the guilty boy with rage.

The boys were terrified of Mr. Stepan, but at the same time we respected him, and even loved him. He was an odd man. Other teachers retired to their quarters to rest, but he spent all of his free time with the older boys. He gathered the teenagers around him, narrating his past adventures. He was almost one of the orphans himself, though his wild, brutal gaze set him apart.

The teachers' passion for their work and their love for us were obvious. Many had been with us since the end of our time in Antoura, and they stayed with us through Aintab and Beirut. They had basically become our surrogate parents, and we treated them as such. Under these tents, we had built a large family together, as cohesive and happy as any in the world, despite the trauma we had collectively endured.

We often spoke of the past. The previous five years had been imprinted indelibly onto our souls. But we had to keep looking to the future. No matter what happened, wherever we ended up, we would continue struggling to keep our Armenian heritage alive, to preserve our very existence. We had to grow into respectable men and restore our nation's honor. We had to become educated, to learn languages and sciences.

"You are Armenians, sons of a great nation," Mr. Stepan told us. "Your parents may have been illiterate, but even they understood the value of education, and besides, they were intelligent and creative people and performed miracles with their hands. Don't forget that you come from a line of great thinkers."

From the caves of Aintab to the tents of Karantina, we held classes with absolute regularity. We might not have had desks, books, or notebooks, but we wanted to learn, to unlock the secrets of the world, to be like bees sucking the nectar of knowledge from its source.

∽

One evening, during dinner, Mr. Travis announced we were moving to the town of Jbeil,* up the coast from Beirut. The news spread quickly, unleashing an outburst of euphoria. We finally would have a permanent home where we could be fed and educated properly, where we could come of age without the threat of bullets, hunger, or beatings.

The next morning, we marched to the train station. Our train sped along the coast, passing familiar towns from our many recent travels. When we reached the terminus of the train tracks, the headmaster arranged for each teacher to lead a group of orphans down the road. A truck would have to make four trips to carry us all to the orphanage. The first group boarded, and those boys waved to the rest of us as the truck pulled away.

The sun leaned toward the western horizon. In the dusk, the surface of the sea shimmered as if covered by a thin veil of gold. The hills were dotted with small villages. Along the road, people stared at our group of ragged orphans in amazement.

---

* Jbeil (Jubayl in Arabic) is the local name for the ancient city of Byblos.

I had to wait for the fourth and final trip to climb aboard. Eventually, we arrived at some ancient ruins in a small village.

"We've arrived. This is Jbeil!" announced the driver. "Look down toward the beach! See? That's where your new home will be." We entered the village, reached its square, and then made a sharp turn, heading toward the beach. Finally, we came to a halt and climbed down. Those who had arrived before us were waiting in a courtyard, whiling away the time with games.

There were more than three hundred boys. Facing us was a large facility with two buildings. One was a solid, imposing two-story structure. The other was smaller, with eight or ten windows, though some of the panes were broken. Portions of the roof were also missing.

We were spending the night in this smaller building. The bedrolls were immediately unrolled on the cold ground. "Don't worry, boys, tomorrow we'll arrange for everything. All will be settled soon," said one of our teachers.

The sun dipped into the sea, and after a small dinner of bread and cheese we went back outside. We walked along a small path lined with trees. Their branches grew in interlocked patterns, forming strange knots. Up the path, we found still more ruins, dotting the valley all the way down to the water. In the dark, they looked eerie and mysterious.

I stood in the twilight near those ruins and reflected on my journey. We had come to a new country, and we would again start from scratch. But we had everything necessary to survive, and we would continue to receive our education. Now, we had to work as hard as possible to rebuild our shattered lives.

AFTERWORD

Keith David Watenpaugh

Karnig Panian's return from Aintab to Lebanon under the French Mandate—and yet another orphanage—marked not just a critical turning point in his own life but in the larger international drive to help Armenians repair their lives and community in the wake of genocide. The American Red Cross had turned Panian's care over to Near East Relief (NER), a massive American nongovernmental aid organization that had taken the lead in addressing Armenian suffering.* NER brought together an older generation of American Protestant missionaries in the Middle East with Progressive-era Americans who had come of age during the Great War. The organization had set for itself the ambitious task of reforming the entire region—an idea encapsulated in the title of its journal, *The New Near East*.

Armenian genocide survivors were at the center of this effort. During the war, the cause of the Armenians had been popular in the United States and NER had raised funds for immediate relief, but after the war was over, it had planned to resettle Armenian refugees in Anatolia, in particular in those parts occupied by France. The organization sent orphans and other survivors from Syria and Lebanon to the cities of Aintab, Urfa, Marash, and Adana. However,

---

* See my *Bread from Stones: The Middle East and the Making of Modern Humanitarianism* (Berkeley: University of California Press, 2015); James L. Barton, *The Story of Near East Relief: An Interpretation (1915–1930)* (New York: Macmillan, 1930).

NER had not anticipated the ferocity of the Turkish nationalist opposition to both the French occupation and the return of the Armenians, and a terrible, multi-sided civil war soon engulfed all of Anatolia (1919–1923). What Panian witnessed in Aintab was reproduced elsewhere, such as the city of Marash, where civil violence led to the massacre of 12,000 Armenians in 1920.

As Panian and other Armenians fled the war in Anatolia, they faced a very uncertain future. They were an overwhelmingly young and female stateless people in a land where the majority of the inhabitants spoke a different language—Arabic—and were generally hostile to their presence. As seen in Panian's own recollection, NER officials such as Ray Travis, who is unique in the history of that organization in that he had fought to defend the Armenians of Aintab, and Stanley E. Kerr, who had worked with the Armenians of Marash, remained with the twice-displaced community as it took shape around Beirut and Aleppo.[*] NER established orphanages, schools, and hospitals for the displaced; it embarked on cooperative lending programs to aid in the purchase of land and the building of homes. Often, as in the case of the orphanage at Jbeil, where Panian lived until he was 15, orphans and other Armenian refugees themselves worked to build these new NER facilities—a fact he recalled with great pride later in life.

NER identified young survivors who were especially bright, like Panian, Antranik Zaroukian (1913–1989), also from Gurin, and Asdghig Avakian, an orphan from the Anatolia village of Körpe, and promoted their education, shaping them for community leadership. Avakian became a leading nurse-educator at the American University Hospital in Beirut and wrote an English-language memoir about her life as a child survivor, *A Stranger among Friends* (1960).[†] Zaroukian's *Men Without Childhood* (1985)[‡] details his at times hilarious, at times sorrowful life in an NER orphanage in Aleppo before he went on to a career as a journalist and poet.

---

[*] Stanley E. Kerr, *The Lions of Marash: Personal Experiences with American Near East Relief, 1919–1922* (Albany: State University of New York Press, 1975).

[†] *A Stranger among Friends: An Armenian Nurse from Lebanon Tells Her Story* (Beirut: Catholic Press, 1960).

[‡] *Mankut'iwn ch'unets'ogh mardik* (Beiruit: Matenashar "Hamazgayin," 1955), translated by Elise Bayizian and Marzbed Margossian as *Men Without Childhood* (New York: Ashod Press, 1985).

Each was successful as an adult, evidence again of the resilient potential of children in the face of genocide. Yet they all tell of other young people who fell along the way and the immense burden they felt they carried as among the last of their natal families. Their surviving family and friends all remember how they periodically suffered under the weight of their memory of what had happened to them as children, and how they fought through that pain.

Of the three, Avakian had the most contact with Americans and American institutions throughout her life. Indeed, she is an example of the *real* impact of the NER's project of making a "New Near East": instead of making new Middle Easterners, NER helped make Armenians who were both modern but still "out of place" in the societies where they found refuge. She did not emigrate, though thousands of others in situations similar to hers found assimilation in Syria and Lebanon untenable, and their transition to Western society made smoother by the education and training provided by NER. Panian and Zaroukian, though they too remained in Beirut, wrote exclusively in Armenian and became part of an autonomous, or perhaps more correctly ghettoized, Armenian community in the logic of the sectarian régime of independent Lebanon.*

Panian was instrumental in the revival of that community. Though he was originally trained as an electrician, the love of books and reading and the flair for teaching he first demonstrated at the orphanage in Aintab led him back to school. Later, he became a beloved teacher at the Beirut Djemaran, the premier Armenian education institution in the Middle East. Yet, the refugee Armenian communities in Lebanon and Syria are dying and with them the unique culture of Anatolia's Armenians. Since the genocide, Armenian emigration to the Western Hemisphere, Europe, and what was Soviet Armenia has been constant, but with the outbreak of civil war in Lebanon in 1975, the movement of Armenians became a flood. Beyond the violence and uncertainty of that war, general economic collapse, discrimination, and

---

* On the emergence of a new Armenian intellectual community in diaspora, see Nicola Migliorino, *(Re)Constructing Armenia in Lebanon and Syria: Ethno-Cultural Diversity and the State in the Aftermath of a Refugee Crisis* (New York: Berghahn Books, 2007), 123.

a relative lack of professional opportunities in the Middle East spurred the exodus. Most of Panian's descendants have left the region, as have many of the graduates of the Djemaran itself. And while a small community of Armenians might remain in Lebanon for the foreseeable future, the once immense Armenian community of Aleppo, Syria, which had numbered over 150,000, has now dwindled as a result of Syria's civil war (2011–present) to perhaps fewer than 20,000; many observers believe that a tipping point has been reached and it is no longer viable. At the time of this writing, the extremist Islamist organization, the Islamic State (IS), is poised to capture the city. In places such as Mosul, Raqqa, and Deir al-Zor, the IS has placed severe restrictions on non-Muslims and destroyed important Armenian churches and memorials. There is no reason to doubt that the same would befall Aleppo. Regardless, there just isn't the critical mass of Armenians needed to support institutions like schools, newspapers, and churches that helped preserve the Western Armenian language and way of life of the pre-genocide community in diaspora, and it is only a matter of time before the community Panian helped rebuild dissolves completely in the face of hate, violence, and lack of educational and professional opportunities.

Goodbye, Antoura is an artifact of that community as it faced destruction and then struggled to survive nearly a century ago. But it is also a reminder of how inexorable the process of genocide is once embarked upon by a powerful state and thus how strong the imperative to prevent and punish genocide must be. The cruel project set in motion by men like Jemal Pasha and abetted by Halide Edip continues to exact a terrible price from the children and grandchildren of genocide.

ACKNOWLEDGMENTS
Houry Panian Boyamian

I remember my father as a man not only of great integrity, conviction, and discipline, but also of tremendous optimism and faith. Like so many others who lost their childhoods to great tragedy, he cherished what he had in life, and he committed himself to making that life better. My sister and I grew up feeling his immense love for his children, wife, friends, students, and mentors. But his love for his mother had a special place in his heart, and he honored her memory by dedicating his life to Armenian culture, language, and heritage.

My father did not often talk about his tragic past, but he wrote relentlessly. Besides this memoir of the genocide and the orphanage at Antoura, he wrote about his later experience at the orphanage in Jbeil, about his mentors Levon Shant and Nigol Aghpalian, and about his experiences with the Hamazkayin Armenian Educational and Cultural Society and with Djemaran, the Armenian Lyceum, based in Beirut. He gathered and edited Nigol Aghplian's manuscripts and presided over their publication. He knew how important it was that the world knew about his generation's experiences. He wanted to pass on these stories to those who would follow in his footsteps.

Every April, when the Armenian world commemorated the genocide, he sank into a kind of depression. These may have been the only times that he allowed himself to remember and relive the pain of those years. He died in 1989.

The original manuscript of my father's memoir, which was written in Armenian, was published in 1992. It was published both by the Hamazkayin Armenian Educational and Cultural Society in Beirut, Lebanon, and by the Catholicosate of the Great House of Cilicia in Antelias, Lebanon.

On the occasion of the hundredth anniversary of the Armenian Genocide, my sister, Chaghik Apelian, and I felt a deep obligation to introduce my father's memoir to a wider audience. We hoped to honor the memory of my father and his fellow orphans; to prevent, in our own way, future injustices; and to contribute to the demand for reparations. Therefore, we decided to have the Armenian version translated into English.

I would like to express my gratitude to various people who contributed to the realization of this project. My deep thanks to Khatchig Mouradian, who offered valuable advice as we planned the English translation; Simon Beugekian, who translated the entire manuscript efficiently, thoroughly, and faithfully; Vahe Habeshian, who suggested revisions and wrote explanatory footnotes; Missak Kelechian, who provided photographs of the Antoura orphanage; and Garo Derounian, who provided photographs of the Millet Khan orphanage in Aintab.

I am also grateful to a host of scholars who championed this project. Richard Hovannisian attested to the importance of this memoir, and Vartan Gregorian wrote a heartfelt foreword to the book. Aram Goudsouzian read and edited the initial draft prior to its submission to Stanford University Press, and he provided a thorough revision before its publication. Keith David Watenpaugh was an outstanding advocate for the book, and his introduction and afterword artfully provide the necessary historical context on the Great War and the Armenian Genocide. Kate Wahl, editor-in-chief of Stanford University Press, offered guidance and support throughout the publication process.

Karnig Panian's legacy lives on in the younger generations, including his grandchildren, Annie, Taline, Steve, Haig, and Alik, and his great-grandchildren, Alex, Amelia, Julia, Kyle, and Peter—as well as at least one more child, who will arrive in this world at about the same time as this memoir's publication. I hope that this book conveys to them the strength and determination that my father exhibited throughout his life.